A Roadmap for Teaching Social Media:

All the assignments, rubrics, and feedback guides you'll need to present a strategic social media course

Karen Freberg, Ph.D.

D1366784

DEDICATION

I would like to thank my family for their continued support. Mom, Dad, Kristin, Karla, and Scott have been there encouraging me all the way as I venture on this career as a social media professor. They have supported me with words of encouragement, cups of coffee, and likes and favorites on social media posts I have shared about my class. Mom and Dad have been the best teachers and role models I could have had and their teaching style and view on the profession have shaped me to who I am today. My sisters, Kristin and Karla, both have taught me to bring forth kindness, strength, and humor into my classes and work.

I would like to thank fellow professors in the field who are also teaching social media (Carolyn Kim, Matt Kushin, Emily Kinsky, Ai Zhang, Keith Quessenbery, Amber Hutchins, and Bill Ward) for working with me on various projects and inspiring me in many ways with these assignments. You are all a true inspiration to the field and I have learned a lot from you all based on what you have done for your classes and the success stories you have shared from your students you have had in class.

I would like to thank also all of the students who I have had in class both online and in person at Tennessee, West Virginia, and Louisville. You are all what makes teaching so rewarding and I couldn't' be prouder of the work you have accomplished in and out of class. Your feedback and work makes this all worth it.

Last but not least, I would like to thank three communities on Twitter who really have made a huge impact on my teaching and career. #SMSports, #Hootchat #PRprofs are two of the best communities out there! Such inspirational and wonderful people!

TABLE OF CONTENTS

INTRODUCTION: #HowIGotStarted

One of the great things about teaching is the connection that is formed between the professional and academic community. Public relations is both a research and professional field, and it continues to evolve and adapt to the business environment.

As a professor, I aim to design a course that provides students with a comprehensive, yet succinct, introduction to the new expectations and requirements being made for young social media relations professionals presently. I do think that the phrase "the toughest soldiers come from the toughest schools" sums up my teaching philosophy. If school was always easy-- what would students be able to take aware from their college experience?

I would rather have students come into my class willing to learn and to challenge themselves to become more knowledgeable and efficient scholars by the time they leave class. By setting forth my expectations and what other students have done in previous classes, it sets a solid class culture that is build on hard work, dedication, and focus. I try to provide a supportive and encouraging environment both in person and online for my students to have relevant discussions about the class materials and feel comfortable in asking questions on what they need to be doing for internships, job opportunities, and potentially graduate school.

I began teaching social media for the first time as a doctoral candidate at the University of Tennessee during the spring semester in 2011. I was finishing up my dissertation, applying for jobs, and teaching two classes already. When I found out about our department (Advertising and Public Relations) was going to be offering their very first social media class, I jumped on board to volunteer to be the TA for the class. I wanted to have this experience under my belt before I was in my first tenure track position.

During this course, I was able to learn what should and should not be covered in a social media class, what assignments worked and which ones completely were not well received by the students.

Fast forward to the fall semester as I walked into my new office at the University of Louisville. I was hired as an Assistant Professor in Strategic Communications to teach in our StratComm concentration. However, I was also hired to design their first social media class. At first, I thought I was going to be given a syllabus with a book and be told this is the way it needs to be taught. I did not expect to be given full reign and allowed to create my own class.

Essentially, I used myself as a social media professor as a guinea pig to see what assignments were accepted by the students as well as assignments that would impress social media professionals looking to hire the next generation of practitioners in the industry.

I realized talking with professors at conferences and in person that there was a level of frustration related to where the social media curriculum was going and why there were some resources out there for professors to use, but not as much as you would think. Some professors are very generous in sharing their materials, but others are not. Others don't want anyone to steal their "ideas." This is understandable, but everyone can steal your idea, but they can't steal your brain.

In order to advance the field of social media education, we have to share resources and bounce off ideas.

In 2013, I was able to construct a course that was dynamic, interactive, and combined both research and practice for students to get experience in the area. I have taught the social media class utilizing innovative assignments, program partnerships with companies like Hootsuite and was one of the early adopters to incorporate Hootsuite Higher Education program into the curriculum, utilizing social media to engage and converse with professionals and students online (Twitter), and had the class featured in the popular press (local and national news) as well as several online publications.

In addition, this course has been adapted and used as an example for other social media classes around the nation and even internationally. I was quite honored to see this and it was during this time I realized – more professors needed these resources. I also was able to have a lot of conversations with students as well around the nation and world. Some mentioned to me they wished they had a social class at their university, and they would follow along with my class virtually and participate from afar with the class hashtag. Another example of why I wanted to start this new project.

Teaching social media is a lot of fun. It's one of my favorite classes to teach and inspire students to pursue a career in. Social media has given me many opportunities personally and professionally. It is a class everyone wants to teach, which is why we are seeing so many classes being implemented across the country and around the world.

What I have here is a starting point and framework for a social media class. To give you all fair warning, this is not a class that can be just "implemented" lightly. This is one of the hardest and most demanding classes to teach. There is a constant expectation for you to be on the pulse of what is going on in the industry and establishing your class as the one that best prepares students with creative applied practices, emerging technologies, access to professionals, and practice with innovative tools.

This industry is constantly changing, so the assignments and syllabi have to as well. You will be working twice as hard (maybe even three times as hard!) in this class compared to others due to the constant prep, demand, and changing of your class to meet the expectations for your program and university. With that being said, the work and dedication you have for the class will bring forth numerous opportunities for your students as well as for yourself as the professor professionally.

The purpose of this assignment book is to provide professors and students the opportunity to learn about social media from an applied and strategic angle. I wanted to create a resource I wish I had in my hands as a young assistant professor embarking in a new class. I also wanted to provide a resource where a student could do these exercises on their own and create content that would be appropriate to include in a portfolio or work sample piece for a job application or internship.

We are all in this together and on the same team. We can all learn from each other when it comes to teaching social media.

There are many wonderful books and resources out there on the subject, but none that really focus on how to apply these principles into work that can be used to gain internships, jobs, and press as a social media professor. I hope you find this book to be enjoyable, useful, and helpful as both a teacher and student.

I would love to hear your suggestions and feedback on this ebook. This was a product of many hours brainstorming during writing and workout sessions, thinking over coffee, and chatting with many great professionals in the education and public relations profession.

Thank you and enjoy this ebook focusing on teaching social media!

Best Wishes,

1 GETTING STARTED

Before embarking on the task of creating new assignments and lectures, there are certain things you want to make sure you do to focus on the tactical aspects of making a social media class successful. These next few steps will help you build a foundation for what is expected for a professor or student in this class.

BUILDING THE SOCIAL MINDSET

Many professors and students have reached out to me to ask how they can get into the mindset that is needed to be successful in a social media class. The rest of this chapter should give you some hints about getting prepared to teach your first social media course.

Be aware, teaching social media is not like any other classes you have already in your toolkit as a professor.

JOIN THE COMMUNITY

You first have to BE on social media to teach social media. I am not saying you have to be on every single platform, but you want to be at least part of the major ones. I have found Twitter to be the best when you are looking to reaching out to people you WANT to meet. However, LinkedIn and Facebook are different communities, and this is where you can create some interactions in selected or invited groups. In addition, you want to consider if there is one platform you want to experiment around with and see what works and what doesn't.

For example, I did this with Snapchat in 2015 and I thought it would be good to determine if this would be one platform I would want to use for the classroom. It was not until I saw the power of the stories and engagement I had within the sports community I fully embraced this platform. There is no right or wrong answer here to which platforms to join, but it does come down to what fits your own interests and ideas, and the audience and community to are trying to reach and engage with.

So, you have decided the platforms you want to be on, but where to next? First, you want to set out and get some resources on each of these platforms. Luckily, there are many different guides out there for you to look at to get an idea of how to strategically use each of these platforms for your own brand. Mashable has a guide for every platform, so if you go and search on their website "Snapchat guide," you will get a lot of articles. In addition, going to Hootsuite, Buffer, and SproutSocial would also be highly recommended. They have quick articles to help you get started as well as free guides and white papers to download.

Second, once you download these guides, think about where you want to go and how much time you want to dedicate to being online. Set up a time you feel would be manageable (10-15 minutes a day) you would want to spend building your presence on each of these platforms. You do NOT have to be on social media 24/7. Yet, you want to be consistent with the updates you want to share on each of these platforms. If you are consistent for a few months and drop off, this is where the problems can arise.

Be kind to yourself for the first few weeks. It will take time to get started on this journey and you want to do a little bit each day. As each day goes forward, it gets easier and we have a great community of #PRprofs who are happy to answer any questions (including me!).

ESTABLISH YOURSELF WITH CONFIDENCE
First, build self-confidence and project that you KNOW what you are doing. If you walk into the class with any self-doubts, the students will be able to read that in a heartbeat. Students already have certain stereotypes about what a "professor knows" about social media, and they're usually not positive.

Confidence in social media does not happen overnight. It takes time and dedication to build your community and reputation.

First, as mentioned in the previous section, you want to start small and continue to build on these skills. Start off the first few weeks seeing what is working for you and what is not. Ask fellow professors you know who are actively engaged on social media and get their feedback on what they see on their end. It's always good to get others to see what you are doing and what you may want to consider doing as well.

However, you want to make sure you are aligning with how you are offline as well. One of the biggest challenges we see in the social media world is inconsistency between an online persona and how this person is offline. You want to act the same – one set of manners and persona.

CREATE AN ENGAGED LEARNING ENVIRONMENT

With that being said - set the tone for the class by stating you are willing to learn from them as well. There are going to be some things your students will know and experience that you may not be aware of or know about.

That's okay. In fact, use student expertise as an opportunity to provide them with a way to showcase these skills for their fellow classmates. Integrate a day of workshops led by your students to educate their fellow classmates.

For example, in 2016, Snapchat launched the opportunity to create their own geofilters based on a certain location. One of my students, Danielle, said they LOVED Photoshop and actually took the initiative to create our very first class geofilter for #Freberg16. I was so impressed by this I asked Danielle if she would like to do a dedicated workshop on how to create a geofilter for the class.

She became the professor of the day and the students were thrilled with this. In fact, many of the students took this lesson and applied it into their final class project and even used it for internship and job interviews. This showed me we are all part of this journey together.

So, if you have a student in class who is your resident expert on Snapchat. Reddit, or any other platform or strategy, you may want to give them the microphone for the day and become a teacher to their fellow classmates.

Teaching others and mentoring future scholars is one of the primary roles of all educators. However, educators not only have to be in the role of a teacher, but they can also be a student as well. Educators have to be active listeners and can learn from anyone about a given subject, so we have to be open to the various possibilities. Educators have to keep up with the latest technologies used in public relations and communications (ex. social media), analyze case studies that are occurring in the profession, adapt and refine research skills that are relevant in studying a particular phenomenon, and provide creative and innovative assignments that best prepare the students for the workplace.

I enjoy the class atmosphere and presenting information that is current, relevant, and interesting to students. I believe that public relations students need a combination of exposure to "real-world" situations and the ability to conduct and understand public relations research. In my mind, there is nothing better in terms of learning than hands on experience—both in public relations campaigns and research.

BUILD A ROUTINE
Keeping up with social media requires commitment and time. You want to figure out what works best for you when it comes to the timing of your day. There are going to be some days where you will be able to share, comment, and engage a lot on social media. However, there are going to be some days where you are not as social. That is perfectly fine - you just want to make sure you do check in and are consistent with your presence. In addition, you don't want to over commit on something or a platform and not be able to sustain it.

So, you want to make sure you schedule time each day that is dedicated to reading what is current in your network. Create a list of must go to sites you will read each day and see what is happening in the social media sphere. I use several like Mashable, Social Times, Digiday, The Next Web, Social N Sport, DigitalBuzzMarketing, and Buffer to name a few. Another strategy is to do a Google News search for a particular topic (ex. Snapchat) and see what stories come up. I do this each and every day to catch up on what is happening across the industry.

How much time do you need to do this? Not much. I block out at least 10-15 minutes each morning just for this. I go to my sites, read the articles, and then share the articles I feel are most relevant for my class online. I use a URL shorter (Hootlet), but you can also use Bit.ly to do this as well. I do this for a few reasons: 1) I can schedule these readings to go out at a later time if I want to so I can make sure my students see these updates not at 5 am, but at 11 am if I want and 2) I can track and see how many students actually have opened up the articles to read. It's important to look at the resources people are interested in reading.

2 BRANDING YOUR SOCIAL MEDIA CLASS

There are hundreds of social media classes being offered around the world, so it is important to be able to determine what will make **YOUR** class uniquely yours and different from other classes.

Will it be your assignments? Will it be the partnerships with software or analytics program you have for your class and institution? Or do you have a distinct visual branding template you use for all of your social media posts?

These images are very easy to create, thanks to tools like Canva (where you can create different images based on social media measurements), Adobe Spark Products (mobile apps), and other resources like Photoshop and Illustrator. Personally, I am not as skilled as a graphic design as I would want to be, so these tools are very helpful if you want to create images that look professional.

Professors and professionals talk a lot about personal or corporate branding for companies, students, and our respective academic institutions, but we never consider what OUR brand is for ourselves or even for the classes we offer to our students. This is something we need to think about and address. Plus, we are already teaching the key components of what makes a successful branding campaign, but instead of soaking up this information for ourselves, we are focusing on what others can do with these insights. The time has come to embrace personal and professional branding for our social media classes and be able to share this with others at the local, national, and international level.

These are all questions you will need to consider in terms of how you present your class, how you will be marketing it on campus for students and fellow colleagues, and how to gain awareness in the local, national, and global community.

SO – WHY IS BRANDING YOUR CLASS KEY TO YOUR SUCCESS?

Along with your research articles and grant proposals, your teaching this class could also serve as a way to connect with future students and prospective clients. Awareness of your class and its students can be increased among future employers and graduate school faculty and programs.

In addition, agencies, professionals, and businesses are looking for the best talent to join their communities and companies, so they want to be aware of what makes your class different compared to others. Coming up with a professor and class brand will set you apart.

I NEED TO BRAND MYSELF AND CLASS – WHERE TO START?

Embrace your uniqueness and be your own brand
While it is tempting to try to be like someone else who is teaching a social media class, you have to do what is most comfortable for you. Experiment to determine what your social media voice is and how you want to communicate this as part of the class.

Look at what other professors are doing and determine 1) what practices and strategies do you like, 2) what practices and strategies need revision before you feel comfortable doing them in your class and 3) what NEW things can you could bring to the table that have not been done befor. Be an explorer and experiment with different assignments, tools, and programs.

Conduct a SWOT analysis for your class brand (see Class Branding Audit Document)

To determine where you are and where you want to be, you want to make sure you are aware of what other professors are doing for social media classes.

Second, you will want to conduct secondary research into social media syllabi to determine results in the following categories:
- Textbook (Assigned or Not)
- Readings (additional resources, etc)
- Assignments
- Teaching Awards (University / Professional Associations)
- Reviews
- Speaking at Teaching and/or Social Media Conferences
- Popular press interviews and mentions
- Guest speakers
- Certifications and Program Associations
- Professor on Social Media (what tools are they using, branded hashtag for your class like #COMM333 (if this is your class title) or personalize it to be your name like #Freberg16 as I have done, or a mixture of the two like Ai Zhang of Stockton University has done with #AZSM.)

Once you figure out how others have branded their social media classes, you will need to compare the skills you have and areas you may need to work on for the class. You will want to do this before each semester you are teaching a social media class.

I do this the fall semester before I teach my social media class (always offered in the spring semester) so I know who is leading and what areas and gaps I need to address. For example, I noticed one year I only spent two days talking about digital and social media analytics, which I knew I had to address and make sure I spent more time on it for my students. From teaching the social media class in spring 2015 (spending two days on social media analytics) I made changes to the class for Spring 2016 (where I spent two weeks) on the subject. You have to look at the field and ask yourself: What are the key areas I need to cover and what are some areas I can let go? I used to have a lot of time spent on specific platforms at the beginning of the semester, but I have condensed this down to an overview of each platform for a day.

Your class is not just about the branding tools, but branding mindset
This is one of the things that gets complex when teaching a social media class. We always think about the tools that need to be covered and what textbook we will be using. These are tactical

branding elements, but professors and fellow educators have to think about the branding mindset. What behaviors and actions do you want students to take away that are uniquely different from other students coming out of different programs? What are some of the things you want to make sure your students walk away with not only in terms of skills, but a mindset? These are things you want to make sure to address and frame for your class and students ahead of time. For example, when I was a graduate student in PR at the University of Southern California, their branding mindset was all about strategic creative thinking. We were drilled in class each and every day about the following: What is the "so what?" factor? What are the gaps here and what are ways we can be creative in our applications based on this information?

Determine what your class hashtag will be
There is no best practice or right answer to this. However, you want to make sure if you do choose to use your class number (ex. COMM 333), that it is not taken already. Many professors have done this, or they have incorporated their last name (or initials) to the hashtag to personalize it more to their class at the respective universities.

I decided to go with my last name because 1) the class name COMM 333 was already taken and 2) not many professors have my name, I have gotten reactions from other professors to see if this was a bit over the top because I am saying it is "my" class. My response is – no, not really, because it is the students who are making the class the way it is. The only thing I change each year is the year in the hashtag. Each class has ownership of their class hashtag experience, but all students who have completed my class are alums, or otherwise known as #FrebergAlums.

Once you have created your hashtag for the class, you will want to use it for your social media updates to gain awareness of the class and integrate it into your visuals. Canva (available online and the app store) and Adobe Post (app store) have specialized features which will allow you to do this.

Colors and other visuals tell a story too
Color is an important factor, and you want to make sure you are consistent with the colors, font, and overall size of the font you will

be using in your branding for your social media class. Canva is a great tool to create images, posters, and social media updates for your class to help with the branding for your class.

What I like about Canva is the fact you are able to get the logos of the main social media platforms and present them in a professional manner.

While this is just one option, you will want to explore also the possibilities of mobile apps like Word Swag and Adobe Post as well to help create social media updates and visuals directly from your smartphone and tablet.

Visual content should be created and integrated throughout the class if you are using a blog for managing your classroom discussion or another social media platform (ex. Twitter).

Class materials are the first place you can integrate your class branding.

- *Syllabus*: Create a header for the class with your branded hashtag. These can be created very easily in Canva.
- *Assignments*: This provides some consistency with the overall materials for the class to have a consistent heading and presence as well with the assignments.
- *Lectures*: Have the class hashtag branded on each slide for each class presentation.
- *Guidelines and Etiquette Policies*: Consider if you want to integrate the branding for the class in your email signature (Wisestamp is a good tool for this if you are integrating or using Outlook).

Here are some examples of visuals you can create for the class:

- *Social media updates related to class.* You want to make sure to provide some visuals along with your updates related to class (ex. Cancelled class, weather delay, etc) so it is consistent with the overall branding of the image.

  These can be shared across your platforms as well as integrated into longer form of content like blogs and articles.

- *Snapchat filters*: You can create a filter for a specific guest speaker, event, and assignment for the class and share this with other platforms. These can be created via Canva or Photoshop, or when you sign into your account online, they have downloadable guides for you to use as an example for creating one for your class.

- *Workshops and Presentations.* If you will be doing presentations and workshops for class, these are also opportunities to reinforce the branding of your class visually.

- *Motivational quotes:* You are building a community within your class with your students, so you want to make sure you inspire them in and out of the classroom. Motivational quotes and other quotes that spark creativity and humor related to the class would also be appropriate.

- *Announcements for Assignments:* Reminders to the class about what assignments are due and when is going to be something to consider addressing here as well. These can be created ahead of time using tools like Canva and Adobe Post. You can schedule these images and updates to go out at certain times during the course of the semester.

- *Announcements for Guest Speakers:* Making an announcement (similar to what you see at conferences and webinars) for guest speakers is another way you can brand your social media content for your class.

Overall, there are many different ways you can brand yourself and your motto / class. You just want to make sure you are distinct and unique compared to other class offerings and what you offer is based on your own unique values, traits, and voice characteristics for your class.

3 CREATING YOUR OWN CLASS ETIQUETTE AND SOCIAL MEDIA POLICY

Having an etiquette (or netiquette) policy for a social media class is essential. You want to make sure to stress for your students that professional email and social media correspondence is both a key factor and component not only for this class, but also for future job prospects after graduation. Setting a good first impression with your email and social media writing is key.

You want to make sure your students (and yourself) treat each email, tweet, snap, and update as you would if you were working at an agency or for a brand. Today, it's essential to have strong social media (http://www.smartbrief.com/original/2014/09/how-mind-your-manners-social-media) and email etiquette skills (http://www.slideshare.net/kfreberg/student-email-and-social-media-etiquette-policy-for-freberg15).

I have attached as part of this assignment as an example of my social media and email etiquette policy, but here are some points I have found to be useful:

- Public Forum: We will be using social media for our outside class participation, so this is a public forum for everyone and ANYONE can read your tweets. Be aware of these before you tweet, update, or snap for class.

- Respect: Be respectful and professional toward everyone in class, including the professor.

- Be respectful to ALL guests coming into class: Whether these professionals are in person or visiting via Skype, it is important to give them your full attention and be on time to class. Do not show up late because it causes disruption to the class and shows a lack of respect for the guest speakers, who is taking time out of their busy schedules to share their expertise, insights, and thoughts with you.

- <u>Check spelling and grammar:</u> Make sure you are double-checking the spelling and grammar for all of your updates, even the class hashtag. Otherwise, we will not be able to see your tweets related to the class.

- <u>Live tweeting or updating in class:</u> Unless specified, you should not be on your phone and on social media, especially when we have guest speakers unless the guest speakers say it is okay or the professor says it is okay. If you are on your phone during class time and not paying attention to the course material, you will 1) miss out on important information related to the class and 2) this will show disrespect to your fellow classmates, the professor, and the guest speaker.

- <u>Timing:</u> I will try to respond in at least 24 hours to email and maybe a few hours at the most for social media updates. Don't 1) forward me your email if I have not responded in an hour, 2) email and tweet me about the same questions – I will answer in one format or another depending on the scope of the question and 3) Don't expect an immediate answer if you are tweeting an immediate concern at 3 am – I will respond to this later in the morning.

4 INVITING GUEST SPEAKERS TO CLASS

One of the more rewarding activities for social media classes is to get professionals who are working in the industry to come to your class and share their insights and expertise with your students. Having guest speakers speak to class or virtually offers a great experience for the students to be able to share, bounce off ideas, and learn from those in the workplace and industry. Some of these professional connections can last beyond the classroom setting, and in some cases, make opportunities for the students as they graduate from the university.

If you are not able to get a professional to come to your classroom in person, try hosting a virtual guest lecture. Skype, Google+, and Uber Conference are just a few ways to bring a guest into your class.

Here are some common concerns you may have when it comes to bringing guest speakers to class:

- *Some guest speakers want a speaking fee*: If this is the case, you are better off without them. Most of the time, professionals who ask for speaking fees to speak to a class are not worth the effort.

- *Guest speakers want to speak on certain topics, and only those:* Be aware that there are some speakers who want to be the guest speaker for one particular topic. If they are an expert in this area, that is great, but if not – then you may want to see if they'd be willing to chat about another topic.

- *Looking at the treatment they give to you and your class:* Pay attention to how they engage others. Some professionals are very good with students, and others not so much. Be mindful of this when you are sending out your invitations to your class.

Where to begin
I am a big fan of Jane Austen books, and I have always said if the characters just communicated, all would be fine. The same goes

with guest speakers. If you want to have someone speak to your class, reach out to them. Professionals WANT to speak to classes! You also have alumni from other classes and programs you may want to reach out to as well. You want to have a balance of in person speakers and virtual speakers for your students.

Make sure to think about the type of speakers who would benefit your students. Consider adding a bit of local, national, and even international caliber talent to your classroom.

The best thing to do is contact potential speakers via email or through social media (ex. Twitter). You may want to start this a few weeks before you actually begin teaching the class to make sure you have enough guest speakers for your class for the following semester.

Along with your email, you may want to share your syllabus with the professional coming into your class. This will give him or her an idea of what you will be covering for the class. Plus, they can provide some additional feedback for you for your class from their point of view, which is always helpful.

Essential social media questions for your guests
Ask whether or not it is okay for students to live tweet or update the lecture. Some professionals are okay with this, but others are not. You as the professor need to clarify and communicate their preferences to your students.

If the guest speakers are okay with sharing, make sure to share updates on the social media platform you are using to announce that these individuals will be coming to your class to speak on a certain topic. Make sure to provide the hashtag for your class (if you are using one) for your guest speakers so they are able to share with their respective followers and community members.

Template for Contacting Potential Guest Speakers

I have found email and Twitter to be the two best ways to get in touch with guests about a possible guest lecture for my class. Here's an email template I have used for engaging guest speakers. Obviously, you would want to put this in your own voice.

Hello [Name],

I hope you are having a great day so far. I wanted to reach out to you about possibly coming to my class as a guest speaker? Your expertise in the area of [subject] would be wonderful for my students to hear.

Anyway, my class meets from [time] in Room and location. I have reserved a parking pass for you in the visitor's lot [see if you can arrange this with your university and make sure to provide a link to the campus map for them to look at]. I have all [provide an overview of the type of students you have, their majors, interests, etc for the speaker to get an idea of the audience they will be talking to for your class]. If you need a computer or any tech equipment, please let me know [may also want to chat with your IT department to see if they can help here as well.]

I will have my cell on me tomorrow as well if you have any additional questions. Let me know if you have any additional questions. Thanks and hope you have a great evening! :)

Before the classroom guest lecture, you want to make sure to:
- Have a preliminary meeting and test the call ahead of time. You want to make sure the guest is comfortable with the technology and that you can address any issues that may happen ahead of the class time.
- Go over the time the class is in session. This is key so they can see if they need to prepare for a 50 minute lecture or a 1.5 hour session.
- Ask permission to give materials from their presentation to the students.
- Have a plan B. Sometimes the Wifi in the classroom is not working or the connection is not strong on the other side. Make sure to go over these plans with your guest ahead of time so there is no confusion on both sides.
- Make the announcement to your class offline and online. You will want to encourage them to do their research on the guest speaker before they arrive in class so they are prepared. Have them read their blog, articles they have written, video interviews, and see what they are posting on various social media platforms.

- Go over proper guest lecture class etiquette with the students – what they need to do when the guest is in class, etc.

During the guest lecture
- Start off class with a brief overview and introduction to the guest speaker for your students. You can provide them with the live tweeting assignment for the guest speaker (see Guest Speakers as a guide.
- Monitor social media updates (if this is okay with the guest speaker) and share these with your respective followers
- Take pictures for the session and share across appropriate social media platforms.
- Encourage students to thank the guest for his or her time and for sharing insights with the class.
- Provide a thank you card and small giftcard for the guest speaker for their time. Make sure the thank you note is personalized and tailored for the guest and lecture.

It was awesome skyping with @chriskerns in the #Freberg15 class! Learned a lot about social analytics and what goes on behind a tweet.

11:51 AM - 13 Feb 2015

@kfreberg this is a great addition to @chriskerns lecture today. I never imagined statistics could be so fascinating. #Freberg15

1:15 PM - 13 Feb 2015

S/o to @chriskerns for speaking to #freberg15 this morning. So fascinated with how he uses data! #sm #analytics

11:07 AM - 13 Feb 2015

After the guest lecture

- Write your own summary of the talk. This could be on your own personal blog or it could be a post on LinkedIn. Social currency is what a lot of professionals look for and this can be used for their own resume, CVs, and updates as well.
- Curate any social media updates the guest speaker has shared with their followers and any that mentioned your class.

- Create a Storify of the social media content that was posted and shared during the timeline of this guest talk.
- Share social media updates and feedback with your guest speaker. Ask your students (for extra credit if they are interested) to write a blog post reflecting their thoughts about the guest on social media.
- Ask for feedback from the guest speaker: If this is someone you would like to have back in your class, ask them what they liked and what are some things they wish to be improved next time.

5 SETTING UP A CLASS HASHTAG

One of the things you will want to make sure to do if you are going to be teaching a social media class and using Twitter is to create a social media class hashtag.

This way, it will be easy for you to keep track of the conversations in and out of class. However, before you start tweeting for your class, you want to make sure to set up some guidelines and expectations.

Many classes have used Twitter to share articles and resources, but you want to create a great and dynamic community for others to participate in over the course of the semester. You want to provide students a guide for what type of content you are looking for, but also give them the opportunity to share resources and chat about topics they find relevant and interesting to the class. It's important to have a balance of professional and personal engagement and content creation AND curation for Twitter especially.

Here is an example of what I have done for one of my social media classes with my class Twitter policy:

TWITTER FOR CLASS
The official hashtag for this class on Twitter will be **#Freberg16**. You will need to save this and follow the class feed on Twitter. Checking is a requirement because I will be sharing articles, announcements, internship opportunities, etc. on Twitter for the course that will appear ONLY on the micro blogging site. I'd recommend using either Hootsuite (www.hootsuite.com) or Tweetdeck (http://tweetdeck.com) to follow these conversations and hashtags. Additional conversations and interactions will be conducted on social media. This will be part of your participation grade for this class.

In addition to following the announcements for the class, each student is required to engage and share relevant content on Twitter every week. You will be asked to create **three** relevant tweets each week to the topic covered for the week and respond to **three** of your classmates on Twitter as well on their updates.

When required, your tweets need to 1) fit the max of 140 characters, but aim for 120 characters so you can RT/MT it for your followers; 2) include a link to a relevant video, article, or report to the topic for the week and 3) credit the source of article/report/video by Twitter handle (ex. if you are referencing an article from AP, then make sure to use @AP), and 4) if applicable, make sure to provide a relevant visual to illustrate the concept further (but note this will take up some of your 140 characters).

Twitter Policies: You will need to make sure to follow the guidelines for this class here:

http://www.profkrg.com/courses/class-twitter-policies?utm_source=buffer&utm_campaign=Buffer&utm_content=bufferd4464&utm_medium=twitter. Some to keep in mind for this class in particular: make sure to always use the hashtag, quote correctly your source, use links, spread knowledge, use your manners, engage, and add value to the conversation for class.

You will also need to make sure you are sharing your weekly blog posts as well on Twitter with the class hashtag.

Proposed Topics for the Semester

Week	Weekly Tweet Topics
1	Introduction to Class / Share Interests / UofL standing
2	Social media is like [metaphor] Participate in #FollowFriday
3	Online reputation management (links to articles) & tips Participate in #FF
4	Must follows for #socialmedia & why Participate in #FF
5	Resources for social media Participate in #FF
6	Good social media plan & why Must follows for #socialmedia in terms of agencies
7	Blogging tips for #sm students
8	Hootsuite Certification Program #Instagram tips
9	Social Media Research & Monitoring tips and tools
10	Find a relevant #Twitter Chat related to #socialmedia
11	Crisis cases using social media / crisis pros to follow
12	Examples of New Emerging Media

You do not have to follow me on Twitter (@kfreberg), but you will need to let me know your Twitter handle so I can see you get points for participation online. Make sure your content in appropriate since it is public.

Resources for Twitter

- Writing for Twitter (Guidelines): http://goinswriter.com/twitter-tips-for-beginners/
- Tweetable Tips for Newbies (Shonali Burke): http://shonaliburke.com/18-tweetable-twitter-tips-for-newbies/
- Scientific Guide for writing headlines for Twitter (Buffer App): https://blog.bufferapp.com/a-scientific-guide-to-writing-great-headlines-on-twitter-facebook-and-your-blog
- Twittonary (dictionary for Twitter terms): http://twittonary.com/
- Twitter Dictionary Guide: http://www.webopedia.com/quick_ref/Twitter_Dictionary_Guide.asp
- AllTwitter Terms to know: http://www.adweek.com/socialtimes/the-essential-twitter-dictionary/33288?red=at

6 CONTENT CREATION FOR CLASS

Most employers today expect young professionals to not only share relevant content online on their own social media accounts, but also create content as well. They want to see individual perspectives, voices, and critical thinking skills on subjects and cases impacting the field.

One of the more established forms of online media among advertising and public relations professionals is a blog. You are already getting students started with tweeting and short social media content messages, but they need to be able to write in long form as well. Some have even considered blogs to be more like traditional media.

However, as a professor, I would strongly recommend setting a blog up yourself if you haven't done so already. Students react if they see an assignment they have to do and the professor doesn't have to do it, too. Medium, WordPress, and Blogger are just a few platforms that are very user friendly (and FREE!) and easy to set up. You want to make sure you understand what they are going through in this assignment, and also it provides an outlet for your own content creation as well (helping your overall reputation as a social media professor).

If you decide on blogging as a key assignment for your class, below is a guideline on how to set up this assignment for your class. It is a lot of writing for the students, but they need to have the skills to be able to write more than 140 characters. Writing across mediums and channels is becoming one of the most important skills for young professionals entering the social media era workplace.

Guidelines for Blogging in Class

For this semester, you will be creating your own personal blog where you will be asked to write posts relevant to course material, current events happening in the industry, and other topics of interest to you.

Blogs should be an interactive, current, and engaging platform where you can show and demonstrate your visual, written, and creative expertise about a particular subject of interest. This is also a place where you are sharing your insights and education with the online community.

These blogs should allow you to showcase your knowledge and experience in Advertising and Public Relations, while also reflecting a positive, energetic, and dynamic reputation as a young professional / student.

Here are some tips to note about blogging:

- Make sure your posts are professionally written – grammar and spelling are key since they will be the first thing people use to judge you.
- Make sure to share the blog posts with the class (use Bitly to shorten the URLs of the posts) on Twitter / Facebook (or a platform that is designated for the class on another platform) and attach the hashtag to the update as well on Twitter.
- Make sure to **reference the articles** and pictures / videos you use in your blog post. You will need to have at *least three hyperlinks to articles or videos in each of your blog posts*.
- Blog posts should be **no more than 500 words.**
- Be generous with your insights and information – make sure to include links to articles, videos, reports, and podcasts that enhance and support your points in your post.
- Have a title for your post that is unique, creative, and catches the attention of your reader to go on to your post.
- Tag your posts with key search terms – if you are writing about a particular subject (ex. social media and ethics), make sure that you tag your post with these key terms so they appear in search engines.
- **REMEMBER - You cannot use copyrighted material**. You can only link to content.

As far as the assignment goes, it is up to you on how many posts you want the students to write. Here is what I have my students do for my social media class:

You will be asked to write **two blog posts** a week. You are more than welcome to write more if you would like. **Extra credit** will be noted for students who write blog posts that are related to the guest lectures for this class (review syllabus for schedule):
- **One post** will be dedicated to a social media topic or trend we are either discussing in class for that week or you find interesting related to Strategic Communications.
- **The other post** will be dedicated to what you are either passionate about or interested in (ex. particular industry, hobby, non-profit cause, etc). The topic is up to you – but be aware that what you post on your blog is available to be viewed publicly for others to see.

Some ideas to consider for blog posts:
- Lists (ex. best social media resources or must follows for PR on social media)
- Best practices (tips for Instagram, Vine, or another social media platform)
- Case studies
- New resources or emerging trends

You have to **complete your two blog posts and share them via Twitter using the class hashtag # by [deadline]**. Lateness or failure to produce a blog post for the week will be noted and point deductions will be made.

You will need to:
- Provide me with your blog URL from Twitter by using the class hashtag.
- Share each of your blog posts (copy the URL in your tweet update) on Twitter using the class hashtag as well.
- Make sure you are prepared to share these in class each Monday. These will be selected at random, so make sure you have completed these blog posts by the assigned deadline.
- NOTE: You will need to make sure NOT to post two blogs on the same day (ex. Friday right before the deadline). These posts should be done throughout the week.

Blog topics can also be emphasized and tailored for the class as well. You can follow the same guidelines as you have set forth in your Twitter policy, or you can do it a little differently. I try to do the same content and allow students to write at a deeper level in their blogs from some of the resources shared online.

Also, make sure to share blogging etiquette and ethics here as well for them to realize they have to make sure they are transparent and upfront with their views with others. Charlene Li has a great resource here to cite and share with your students:

Blogger Ethics [from Charlene Li, 2004. Retrieved from http://forrester.typepad.com/groundswell/2004/11/blogging_policy. html).

- I will tell the truth.
- I will write deliberately and with accuracy.
- I will acknowledge and correct mistakes promptly.
- I will preserve the original post, using notations to show where I have made changes so as to maintain the integrity of my publishing.
- I will never delete a post.
- I will not delete comments unless they are spam or off-topic.
- I will reply to emails and comments when appropriate, and do so promptly.
- I will strive for high quality with every post – including basic spellchecking.
- I will stay on topic.
- I will disagree with other opinions respectfully.
- I will link to online references and original source materials directly.
- I will disclose conflicts of interest.
- I will keep private issues and topics private, since discussing private issues would jeopardize my personal and work relationships.

Grading Blogs

Let the students know what you consider to be a strong blog post.

On the next page, you will see a rubric I have created for my blogging assignment for my students so they are aware of the main areas I am focusing on for this assignment as well as what makes a strong blog post for the week.

RUBRIC FOR BLOGGING ASSIGNMENT

There are several automatic deductions of blog points to note including:

- Fact Errors (misspellings of names, locations, businesses, brands) = automatic failing grade (20/40 highest grade a student could get).
- Lateness in submitting the blog posts after the deadline = automatic letter deduction (- 2 points)
- Not sharing blog posts on Twitter using the class hashtag = - 5 points.

	D or below [Unsatisfactory]	C [Satisfactory]	B [Proficient]	A [Exceptional]	SCORE
Content and Creativity [10 points]	Postings show no evidence, research, or additional insights to the topic being discussed. No reflective thought about the topic.	Postings provide minimal insights and understanding on topic. Little reflection and creativity present. Provides minimal research and evidence.	Postings provide moderate insight and understanding with integration of creativity interwoven into commentary. Provides moderate evidence and research	Postings provide comprehensive understanding, insights, commentary, and focuses on bringing forth new questions, new ideas, and sparks conversation to extend the discussion in the community. Provides extensive list of resources and evidence.	
Voice of Author [5 points]	Postings do not reflect awareness, understanding, or consideration for audience. Author's POV is not present. Not able to detect author's voice or personality in post. Words are not carefully selected or considered.	Voice is somewhat presence, but not truly taking into consideration of the audience. POV of author is slightly present, but hard to look for. Voice is there, but difficult to separate. Not consistent with present image and branding of blog	Voice is present and appropriate for audience. Personality is showcased in some parts but not all and the author attempts to bridge commentary with information. POV is integrated somewhat in the post.	Voice is strongly presented throughout the post and done in a professional and integrated manner. Author is very careful in selecting appropriate words to fit commentary and subject. Post comes alive with voice and POV is strongly present.	
Graphics and Visuals [5 points]	Does not insert any images or graphics, images may not be appearing correctly, does not acknowledge source or provide a caption	Inserts graphics and multimedia, but not of high quality. Has some captions, but no hyperlinks and not for all sources	Inserts graphics and multimedia of high quality, infographics. Has captions for sources.	Selects and inserts high quality graphics with captions and hyperlinks to the sources. Acknowledges all sources of content. Creates own infographic and graphics.	
Deadlines and Keywords [3 points]	Did not update the blog and post on time or share on Twitter	Updates blog before deadline but has two posts coming out at the same	Updates blog before the deadline, but may have posts coming	Updates and shares blog before deadline, makes sure to share on Twitter	

		time on the same day	out on same day at different times. Uses class hashtag for Twitter.	using class hashtag	
Citations / Hyperlinks [2 points]	No citations or image citations	Minimal amount of citations and hyperlinks required (2)	Moderate amount of citations and hyperlinks (5). Provides a reading list for more resources (3).	Extensive amount of citations and hyperlinks to relevant articles, reports, and resources on subject. Provides an extensive amount of reading posts for readers (5+).	
Quality of Writing and Proofreading [5 points]	The writing is confused and/or ungrammatical. The reporting is flawed and may contain major factual errors and/or omissions or may show little concept of basic strategic judgment. Work may miss the deadline.	This grade is for work that indicates a problem in at least one area, such as grammar, diplomacy or strategy. It does not measure up to professional quality but could be saved by revision. Work is incomplete by deadline and/or needs more than minor revision. These messages have weak ideas, concepts or presentation.	Writing is grammatically correct but may lack the sparkle and fine organization of "A" work. The work is turned in by deadline with little or no prompting and needs only minor revisions in such areas as reorganizing, rewriting, reformatting or providing more or better sources. "B" work doesn't necessarily have any errors, but it could be better, often with a stronger topic or subject, a more artistic presentation, better information or improved writing.	This grade is for work of clearly professional quality (publishable or broadcast ready). The writing is clear and well-organized; presentation and nearly flawless writing.	
Grammar and Spelling [5 points]	Many grammatical and spelling errors, punctuation errors, and text message lingo. Style does not facilitate professionalism or effective communication	Minimal grammar and spelling errors. Style is more conversational and may distract from the reader.	Writing is relatively grammar-spelling error free, may have some punctuation issues.	No grammar or spelling errors. Strong writing that helps facilitate strong communication and dialogue.	

TOTAL SCORE

PROFESSOR COMMENTS:

7 MANAGING ONLINE REPUTATION ASSIGNMENT

This assignment is one of the most eye opening and relevant assignments you can offer for your social media class. Most of the time, students are somewhat aware of what they are posting to their friends, snapping, etc. However, if they were able to look at this from a different standpoint and see how they are presenting themselves online, this could be a great educational exercise for them.

This could potentially be assigned at the end of the semester, but I look to assign this particular exercise midway through the semester. They can see what they have done so far in the class, but they also have room to improve their overall social media presence and work on their online reputation and brand.

Here is what I have done for my social media class when it comes to their managing online reputation audit assignment:

Managing Your Online Reputation

One of the important elements in being a social media professional and practitioner is not only being aware of your corporate or business online presence, but also being aware of your own online presence as an individual and professional in advertising and public relations.

For this assignment, you will be asked to write a reflection paper (**3-4 pages max**) covering the following material:

- **Overview:** Discuss your overall goals for your online reputation management practices for this class and beyond.
    - Some examples can be establishing credibility and trust as a resource in social media community on specific topic or industry, engaging in online community by sharing expertise and knowledge, get mentions and other references to blog from

others, managing proactive reputation to obtain a job after graduation, etc.
- Make sure to state specific objectives that you have set in regards to your online reputation management efforts not only for this class, but after the class (ex. internship opportunities, jobs, graduate school, etc).

- **Personal Reputation Online Overview:** Discuss and analyze your online bio presented through social media sites – blog, Facebook, Twitter, LinkedIn, Pinterest, Snapchat / Instagram, YouTube, etc. This includes providing the bio that you list yourself on each of these sites. This can be visualized through a table in your paper.

- **Online reputation monitoring and analytics**: Reflect on your overall traffic and mentions on blog posts, Facebook, Retweets, Followers on Twitter, LinkedIn, Instagram, Pinterest, connections, etc.
  - How many mentions have you had on your blog, comments, or site visits over the course of this semester so far?
  - What has been your overall traffic like on your blog since the beginning of this class?

- **Reflections on online reputation building:** Discuss how your blog and the information you are sharing with others through social media is enhancing your online reputation – both personally and professionally.
  - Discuss the characteristics that you consider you possess that has helped build your online reputation (ex. personality characteristics, information sharing behavior, engaging consistently and professionally with followers and others through social media, etc).
  - Think about future trends and goals you have for your online reputation for the rest of the semester and once you graduate, etc.
  - What were your perceptions before and after this assignment in regards to online reputation management?

- **Other:** Items to include in your paper as an appendix: 1) List of profiles on social media 2) Tables and screen shots displaying social media traffic or influence via social media; and 3) Tables listing URLS and Profiles of Social Media Outlets (ex. Facebook / Twitter / LinkedIn /Instagram / Snapchat / Blog).

While managing your online reputation is key, you want to also allow your students to have the opportunity to establish their own personal networking brand. This is one of the things students want to know – how to get connected to professionals and the right people in the industry.

One of the hardest things (and most rewarding) for social media professionals is to establish their personal brand as well as build their own personal learning networks and community. This is a checklist for you all to review, implement, and evaluate during the course.

You will need to be able to discuss, analyze, and apply some of the findings you will be doing for the purpose of this class.

Here is the personal brand checklist you may want to give out to your class to work through and answer. Sharing these insights along with the reputation management paper would be very beneficial and enlightening for the students.

It may also be something professors may be interested in doing for themselves.

SAMPLE PERSONAL BRAND CHECKLIST

1. IDENTIFY YOUR PERSONAL BRAND

- *Who are you as a person?*
  - What is your story? What makes you "you?"
  - What is your background? What are your hobbies and interests?
  - What are key experiences, perspectives, expertise you can bring to the table?

- o What are your strengths and weaknesses?
- o What are steps you are going to take to improve your skills?

- *What is your professional passion?*
  - o What are your personal qualities and characteristics that make you unique?
  - o How are you different from other students taking a social media class?
  - o What are the steps you are going to take to achieve your ideal personal branding statu?
  - o What are going to be the 3-5 topics you will focus on to establish your thought leadership in the community, profession, and on social media?

- **What is your overarching theme or message you want brands, practitioners, and professionals in the industry to know?**
  - o What are your main areas of expertise you want professionals to know you have?
  - o What are three industries/specializations you want to identify in?
  - o Construct your own lists of professionals, brands, blogs, Twitter handles, etc you will want to engage with online.
    - Lists of influencers in the industry you want to work in
    - Lists of agencies, brands, and companies you want to work for
    - Lists of professionals you inspire to be when you graduate
    - Lists of internship / job listings and opportunities
    - Lists of chats to participate in your particular industry

  - o Follow others who are mentioned among those you respect and admire in your community.
    - Brands
    - Professionals
    - Influencers
    - Community Leaders

- Businesses
- Non-Profit Organizations

2. IDENTIFY GOALS AND OVERALL PROFESSIONAL PURPOSE

- *Identify your personal brand voice.*
  - What is your purpose in the field and what can you offer that is different from others?
  - What is the overall tone of your social media voice going to be? What are ways you are going to showcase this to the community?
  - What are the steps you want to take to achieve your goals? Who are the people you want to connect with online who can mentor, educate, and be part of your community?

- *Be aware of professional actions on social media*
  - Be humble and be generous.
  - Think before you post always.
  - Ask feedback and responses from your community. Use Twitter polls for questions if you want.

- *Pay it forward*
  - Think about who you want to reach and by sharing innovative and timely resources, you will start attracting an audience and become listed as a "must-follow" in your community.
  - Practice curation strategies
    - Share each other's work. Best way to get traffic is to increase more exposure and awareness of your work.
    - Give credit to the original users
    - Provide a comment / feedback / takeaway from post
  - Share content such as:
    - Blogs
    - Resources
    - Tutorials
    - Lists of Best Practices

- Slideshares
- Videos / Podcasts

3. ESTABLISHING PERSONAL BRAND

- Visual
  - Create a consistent visual branding of yourself.
  - Same picture / professionalism / cover page / background fitting the platform.
  - Present same bio and voice across social media platforms.

- Content
  - Create, curate, and connect online. Share new content on a regular basis from blogs, websites, news outlets, and relevant chats you participate in.
  - Mix up the content you share. Use Owl.ly / Hootlet to share content in real-time or at a scheduled time/day.
  - Original content needs to be shared too on a regular basis.
  - Mixture of original and curated content is key.
  - Think about what questions, problems, or issues people in your industry want answers to – consider sharing content that could answer these questions or solve these problems. Be a resource

- Engagement
  - Monitor engagement and interactions. See what content is being shared or engaged with more than others.
  - Respond in a timely manner, listen to what they are saying, and implement proper social media etiquette techniques
  - Showcase personality

- Voice
  - Be confident in your voice and perspective while being respective towards others.

- o Monitor and listen to what others say about you. Reflect and analyze on a regular basis.

- Comment and acknowledge content from others
  - o This can be done via quote feature on Twitter.
  - o Images and videos are key. Make sure to include images (personalized through branding sites like Canva) along with your links + comments).
  - o Give out congrats and S/Os

4. STAY INFORMED AND CONNECTED

- Being Informed
  - o Follow relevant brands, industry outlets, and blogs that cover the topics you are interested.
  - o Follow relevant professionals working in the industry you want to work for

- Become connected
  - o Find Twitter chat sessions (ex. #SMSportsChat, #BufferChat, #HootChat) for your respective topics.
  - o Start a dialogue and conversation.
  - o Make it easy to connect and be part of your community.

ESTABLISHING [AND SUSTAINING] YOUR PERSONAL NETWORK

- Sustaining your community connection
  - o Connect with fellow professionals and start the conversation
  - o Read and response/share content from professionals, bloggers, practitioners you respect.
  - o Share relevant, new, and innovative campaigns or resources you feel your network may want to look at.
  - o Seek out mentors in your profession. Connect, engage, and correspond to build professional relationships.

- ○ Give S/Os on a regular basis (not all of the time) but those who you respect and share why
- ○ Give thanks to those who provide you with S/Os
- ○ Conduct virtual introductions
- ○ Find those to you want to mentor and provide help to

- Share blog posts with class hashtag.
  - ○ Post blog post content on LinkedIn Pulse.
  - ○ Comment and share updates you enjoy or want to give a S/O to
  - ○ Share updates on a regular basis, but don't spam/blast them too much

8 SPECIFIC STRATEGY ASSIGNMENTS

You want to provide a wide range of different assignments for your students to practice. One of the favorite assignments I love giving my students is a specific social media strategy assignment.

This allows them to pick a new platform or tool (ex. Snaphat) and propose a way a local business, client, or organization could use the platform or tool proactively.

There are a few things to keep in mind when you are looking at particular strategy assignments:

- *Be very clear on your expectations.* You want to make sure you articulate clearly what you are looking for in this particular assignment.
- *Opportunity for students to test their creativity.* You can state they can't look at what other brands or companies have done.
- *Tie this into multiple ways and approaches.* You can assign this to be part of a client project or individually as well.
- *Provide platform resources for assignment:* With a new platform (ex. Snapchat), you want to add a few references at the end of the paper for additional readings that may be helpful for your students when working on this assignment.
- *This can be tied into a timed exercise.* Sometimes we are asked on the spot what we could do creativity and strategically for a brand using a new platform. This can be easily tied into a timed writing exercise.

This a sample strategy social media brief assignment I created for Snapchat for my social media class to use. Again, this is a template that can be tailored to any new platform you want to use for class.

Overview

Snapchat is a photo messaging app which allows users can take photos, record videos, add text and drawings, and send them to a list of specific users.

You are asked to propose a strategic storytelling brief for either
- Your client for class
- A local business or brand here in Louisville [corporate, small business, nonprofit, event, etc]
- You and how you would use it professionally to get a job with the brand/agency/company of your dreams after graduation from UofL.

Some ideas for how to use Snapchat strategically for a brand (or individual persona) would be by using Snapchat stories (http://www.theverge.com/2013/10/3/4791934/snapchats-next-big-thing-stories-that-dont-just-disappear), promotional videos, contests or sweepstakes, behind-the-scenes footage, selfies, unveiling of new products or campaigns, exclusive content from events, and introduction to team members or VIP guests.

PAPER FORMAT [Max 2 pages single space]
- Introduction to Snapchat [who started this app, statistics of users and how many active users are there on the app, how it's been used, prominent campaigns and brands using app]. Make sure to cite references to these figures.
- Overview of your company/brand: Are they on Snapchat? Is there a rational for them to be on this app? Why or why not?
- Key Audiences (who are you targeting). Demographic and psychographic insights are key to point out here for this particular audience who is not only using Snapchat, but would be relevant to this particular initiative.
- Strategic Mindset (what are key motivational points, interests, trends, and issues you would want to know about your audience – what are they thinking right now?) and what do we want them to think/do after this campaign [call to action steps]. What is the *story* you want to communicate and share with this audience?
- Objectives [what is the overall objective to accomplish with this initiative?

- Storyboard format: What will be the key messages or frames you want to showcase on Snapchat? Create several mock storyboard frames to show how your Snapchat story for this project would look like. An example of a storyboard for Snapchat framework worksheet can be found here from the University of Michigan: http://socialmedia.umich.edu/strategy-guidelines/snapchat-storyboard/.
- Strategies [how are we going to accomplish our objectives?] with what resources and communication tools [tactics]? Make sure to have **at least three strategies** with **two tactics** at least.
- Optional: You are more than welcome to create some snaps for your assignment to showcase your story or propose storyboard snap ideas. Make sure you are considering best practices and proper etiquette when doing these for this assignment. This can be part of your appendix section and not part of the max of two pages.
- Etiquette and proposed best practices for using Snapchat
- References [all in APA style]

Tips
- Make sure you are connecting the audience with the overall goal and application.
- Be creative. Look at the possibilities that are out there for using this particular app for your company or brand you have chosen.
- Be aware of both positives AND negatives of the brand. Consider what are the additional implications and best practices brands and social media professionals have to be aware of when it comes to this app. You may want to address this in proper etiquette as well as maybe suggesting a Snapchat professional guide as well.

Readings

- Marketing Profs: http://ow.ly/BKa4p
- Mashable: http://ow.ly/BKa3p
- How to Succeed with Snapchat Marketing | Social Media Today http://ow.ly/BKadh
- How 12 Brands Used Snapchat | Co.Create | creativity + culture + commerce http://ow.ly/BKarO
- The Beginner's Guide to Snapchat [Mashable] http://ow.ly/BKanU

STRATEGIC BRIEF RUBRIC

When reviewing your strategic brief assignments, you want to make sure to have your rubric in place on what you are looking for in this particular assignment. My template follows on the next page.

RUBRIC FOR STRATEGIC ASSIGNMENT (100 POINTS)

This can be tailored to any of the strategic brief assignments depending on which tool / platform you will want to use for your class.

There are several automatic deductions of blog points to note including:

- Fact Errors (misspellings of names, locations, businesses, brands) = automatic failing grade (20/40 highest grade a student could get).
- Lateness in submitting the blog posts after the deadline = automatic letter deduction (- 2 points)
- Not sharing blog posts on Twitter using the class hashtag = - 5 points.

	D or below [Unsatisfactory]	C [Satisfactory]	B [Proficient]	A [Exceptional]	SCORE
ORGANIZATION & ASSIGNMENT STYLE [10 points]	No organization or structure.	Postings provide minimal insights and understanding on topic. Little reflection and creativity present. Provides minimal research and evidence.	Postings provide moderate insight and understanding with integration of creativity interwoven into commentary. Provides moderate evidence and research	Paper provide comprehensive understanding, insights, commentary, and focuses on bringing forth new questions, new ideas, and sparks conversation to extend the discussion in the community. Provides extensive list of resources and evidence.	
STRATEGIC INSIGHT [30 points]	Insights in paper do not reflect awareness, understanding, or consideration for audience. Author's POV is not present. Not able to detect author's voice or personality in post. Words are not carefully selected or considered.	Insights and understanding of the problem/opportunity for why this strategic brief needs to be created is somewhat presence, but not truly taking into consideration of the audience. POV of author is slightly present, but hard to look for. Voice is there, but difficult to separate.	Strategic understanding and insights are present and appropriate for audience. Ideas are showcased in some parts but not all and the author attempts to bridge commentary with information.	Strategic understanding is strongly presented throughout the post and done in a professional and integrated manner. Author is very careful in selecting appropriate words to fit commentary and subject.	
ALIGNMENT TO GOALS AND OBJECTIVES [20 points]	No alignment or rationale for strategies and tactics. Not connected at all to proposed goals and objectives	Goals and objectives are slightly mentioned, but not fully connected or aligned. Rationale for connection to goals and objectives are not strong but mentioned.	Goals and objectives are somewhat connected, but there are some missing components that could be strengthened. Rationale for why these strategies are connected are good.	Excellent connection and alignment for the goals and objectives. Strategies and tactics fit perfectly within the overall paper and are backed up with strong evidence and rationale.	
CREATIVE CONTENT [10 points]	Does not insert any images or graphics, images may not be appearing correctly, does not acknowledge source or provide a caption	Inserts graphics and multimedia, but not of high quality. Has some captions, but no hyperlinks and not for all sources	Inserts graphics and multimedia of high quality, infographics. Has captions for sources.	Selects and inserts high quality graphics with captions and hyperlinks to the sources. Acknowledges all sources of content. Creates own infographic and graphics.	
CITATIONS AND RESOURCES [10 points]	No citations or image citations	Minimal amount of citations required (3)	Moderate amount of citations (5). Provides a reading list for more resources (3).	Extensive amount of citations and hyperlinks to relevant articles, reports, and resources on subject. Provides an extensive amount of reading posts for readers (10+).	

QUALITY OF WRITING AND PROOFREADING [10 points]	The writing is confused and/or ungrammatical. The reporting is flawed and may contain major factual errors and/or omissions or may show little concept of basic strategic judgment. Work may miss the deadline. Many grammatical and spelling errors, punctuation errors, and text message lingo. Style does not facilitate professionalism or effective communication	This grade is for work that indicates a problem in at least one area, such as grammar, diplomacy or strategy. It does not measure up to professional quality but could be saved by revision. Work is incomplete by deadline and/or needs more than minor revision. These messages have weak ideas, concepts or presentation. Minimal grammar and spelling errors. Style is more conversational and may distract from the reader.	Writing is grammatically correct but may lack the sparkle and fine organization of "A" work. The work is turned in by deadline with little or no prompting and needs only minor revisions in such areas as reorganizing, rewriting, reformatting or providing more or better sources. "B" work doesn't necessarily have any errors, but it could be better, often with a stronger topic or subject, a more artistic presentation, better information or improved writing. Writing is relatively grammar-spelling error free, may have some punctuation issues.	This grade is for work of clearly professional quality (publishable or broadcast ready). The writing is clear and well-organized; presentation and nearly flawless writing. No grammar or spelling errors. Strong writing that helps facilitate strong communication and dialogue.	
TOTAL SCORE					
PROFESSOR COMMENTS:					

9 STRATEGIC MESSAGES ASSIGNMENT

Creating visual content is one thing for social media success, but writing is still one of the most important skills to have as a social media professional. This is one of the reasons why I have my students write A LOT. It gives them practice writing in different formats, mediums, and overall purposes.

I give my students two writing assignments for social media. The goal of both of these assignments is to see if students, given a prompt, can create content for a brand while tying in their overall brand voice. This is one thing a lot of professionals mention as a gap skill missing in the workplace. If you are able to write under time pressure, you will be fine. This exercise can be done in class or at home for the students. They need to be aware of how they would react if they were asked to come up with messages in a short period of time.

One sample assignment for message design (not timed):

Overview of Scenario (can be tailored for local environment / store / event)
You are the representative responsible for the Comfy Cow Ice Cream Store right near the University of Louisville.

The brand in Louisville continues to grow and expand, and one of the ways that the department wants to increase awareness about the program is with new emerging communication platforms such as social media.

You have been asked to come up with a real-time marketing social media initiative for Comfy Cow to position the brand in time for the 2016 Kentucky Derby in May.

Be creative and appropriate for each social media platform. Make sure to provide a reference list to images you used in your social media updates (if applicable) as well.

ASSIGNMENT DETAILS

- <u>Introduction to Client</u>: Provide an overview of the Comfy Cow (2-3 sentences). Evaluate their current use of social media platforms and highlight a few example messages they have created.

- <u>Goal Statement</u>: Think about whether reach, reputation or engagement is your goal. Goals encourage you to be efficient and focused with your social media efforts. Goals will change or expand over time. Understand that each social media application serves different functions dependent upon community members (2-3 sentences).

- <u>Objective statements:</u> Write down <u>three</u> *specific* objectives related to your social media message strategies efforts. Objectives are statements you would like to accomplish during this initiative for the Department of Communication.

  - For example, a goal could be to get more social media mentions of the department, find sources, increase readership, build reputation, find new story angles, etc.
  - Follow the SMART (specific, manageable, achievable, realistic, and time-specific) elements for objectives.

- <u>Audience analysis:</u> Discuss the demographic and psychographic information regarding the key audiences that would be reached (3-4 sentences).

- Write **eight (8)** social media message updates for each platform formatted for the following social media platforms: Facebook (2), Twitter (2), Instagram (2), and Snapchat (2).

  - With each message updates, you will need to provide a rationale and strategy on how you feel this message would be persuasive for the intended audiences, format for the particular social media platform (ex. for Twitter – will you include a link, picture, hashtag, or all of the above for your update?).

- Create at least THREE images to add to your proposed social media updates for Comfy Cow. Images can be created on Canva.
- Consider exploring call to action statements [or call to engagement statements] here for Comfy Cow as well [http://socialnsport.com/callstoengagement/]
- Also note how you will evaluate each of these messages based on metrics. How will you determine if this is a successful message based on each platform?

The next assignment can be done in a certain amount of time. I usually give the students a class time to do this (50 minutes), but this can be tailored and used appropriately for the university, location, and client you are working with.

Prompt for students:
BREAKING NEWS! *The UofL Men's Baseball Team just won the 2016 World Series!*

This is the first time in the school's history where this has been done and we want to make sure to send out social media messages that resonate with fans, community leaders, and students at UofL to help congratulate the team.

Social media messages are most effective if they go out at the right time on the right platform and channel. Your job is to create these images to go out immediately to get the biggest impact among UofL's key audiences as possible. However, you also need to make sure to research and formulate your evaluation of what they have done so far in their social media message strategies before proposing these new ones.

Your deadline to accomplish this is by **11:00 am EST**. You have to submit your work to your boss (in this case, SafeAssign) to review before these are submitted for approval to go live. You have 50 minutes to accomplish this!

Your task is to:

1. Provide a Strategic Brief

- Provide *a strategic brief* (1 page max) going over the background of the team, who is the coach, what are the main platforms you will be using, rationale for each platform, key audiences you are going to reach, and metrics you will be looking at to determine whether or not your messages have been successful, and key audiences for your campaign.
- Provide *an overview of what social media platforms* they are on and ANALYZE them based on their current messages/updates for each platform. What are your recommendations moving forward?

2. Social Media Messages AND Images

- Create <u>four original graphics</u> (two for Instagram and two for Twitter) for the team (a total of *four images*) congratulating the teams on the win.
- *Create four (4) messages* that will go along the lines with each team.
    - Research each team's user handles on both Twitter and Instagram.
    - Take note that 1) Twitter allows only 140 characters and 2) Instagram content only shows three lines of content before showing "…". Keep both of these in mind.

Tips

- Make sure to create these images via Canva. Save them as JPEGs and then copy and paste them into your Word document.
- You need to submit ONE document (strategic brief + images with social media messages) here for this assignment.

Strategic Message Assignment Rubric

You will need to evaluate this assignment the same way you did for your strategic brief assignment. Here is a rubric you can use when grading your social media message strategies assignments:

RUBRIC FOR STRATEGIC WRITING ASSIGNMENT (100 POINTS)

This can be tailored to any of the social media message strategy assignment you have for class.

There are several automatic deductions of blog points to note including:

- Fact Errors (misspellings of names, locations, businesses, brands) = automatic failing grade (20/40 highest grade a student could get).
- Lateness in submitting the blog posts after the deadline = automatic letter deduction (- 2 points)
- Not sharing blog posts on Twitter using the class hashtag = - 5 points.

	D or below [Unsatisfactory]	C [Satisfactory]	B [Proficient]	A [Exceptional]	SCORE
ORGANIZATION & STYLE [10 points]	No organization or structure.	Postings provide minimal insights and understanding on topic. Little reflection and creativity present. Provides minimal research and evidence.	Postings provide moderate insight and understanding with integration of creativity interwoven into commentary. Provides moderate evidence and research	Paper provide comprehensive understanding, insights, commentary, and focuses on bringing forth new questions, new ideas, and sparks conversation to extend the discussion in the community. Provides extensive list of resources and evidence.	
STRATEGIC INSIGHT AND UNDERSTANDING [30 points]	Insights in paper do not reflect awareness, understanding, or consideration for audience. Author's POV is not present. Not able to detect author's voice or personality in post. Words are not carefully selected or considered.	Insights and understanding of the problem/opportunity for why this strategic brief needs to be created is somewhat present, but not truly taking into consideration of the audience. POV of author is slightly present, but hard to look for. Voice is there, but difficult to separate.	Strategic understanding and insights are present and appropriate for audience. Ideas are showcased in some parts but not all and the author attempts to bridge commentary with information.	Strategic understanding is strongly presented throughout the post and done in a professional and integrated manner. Author is very careful in selecting appropriate words to fit commentary and subject.	
ALIGNMENT TO GOALS AND OBJECTIVES [20 points]	No alignment or rationale for strategies and tactics. Not connected at all to proposed goals and objectives.	Goals and objectives are somewhat connected, but they could be stronger and more aligned. Rationale for these strategies and objectives are good.	Goals and objectives are somewhat connected, but there are some missing components that could be strengthened. Rationale for why these strategies are connected are good.	Excellent connection and alignment for the goals and objectives. Strategies and tactics fit perfectly within the overall paper and are backed up with strong evidence and rationale.	
CREATIVE CONTENT [10 points]	Does not insert any images or graphics, images may not be appearing correctly, does not acknowledge source or provide a caption.	Inserts graphics and multimedia, but not of high quality. Has some captions, but no hyperlinks and not for all sources.	Inserts graphics and multimedia of high quality, infographics. Has captions for sources.	Selects and inserts high quality graphics with captions and hyperlinks to the sources. Acknowledges all sources of content. Creates own infographic and graphics.	
CITATIONS AND RESOURCES [10 points]	No citations or image citations	Minimal amount of citations required (3)	Moderate amount of citations (5). Provides a reading list for more	Extensive amount of citations and hyperlinks to relevant articles, reports, and	

			resources (3).	resources on subject. Provides an extensive amount of reading posts for readers (10+).	
QUALITY OF WRITING AND PROOFREADING [10 points]	The writing is confused and/or ungrammatical. The reporting is flawed and may contain major factual errors and/or omissions or may show little concept of basic strategic judgment. Work may miss the deadline. Many grammatical and spelling errors, punctuation errors, and text message lingo. Style does not facilitate professionalism or effective communication	This grade is for work that indicates a problem in at least one area, such as grammar, diplomacy or strategy. It does not measure up to professional quality but could be saved by revision. Work is incomplete by deadline and/or needs more than minor revision. These messages have weak ideas, concepts or presentation. Minimal grammar and spelling errors. Style is more conversational and may distract from the reader.	Writing is grammatically correct but may lack the sparkle and fine organization of "A" work. The work is turned in by deadline with little or no prompting and needs only minor revisions in such areas as reorganizing, rewriting, reformatting or providing more or better sources. "B" work doesn't necessarily have any errors, but it could be better, often with a stronger topic or subject, a more artistic presentation, better information or improved writing. Writing is relatively grammar-spelling error free, may have some punctuation issues.	This grade is for work of clearly professional quality (publishable or broadcast ready). The writing is clear and well-organized; presentation and nearly flawless writing. No grammar or spelling errors. Strong writing that helps facilitate strong communication and dialogue.	
TOTAL SCORE					

10 SOCIAL MEDIA CAMPAIGN

If you are teaching a social media strategy course, you are most likely going to be having a semester long project for the students to work on.

This project in many cases is a social media campaign or a campaign proposal project a group of students work on together over the course of the semester.

This is the first time I have ever openly shared my social media campaign proposal document. This is the one a lot of colleagues, fellow professors, and other professionals have asked me for. This is one of the main takeaways my students gain from my class, and I wanted to use this ebook as an opportunity to showcase this.

This social media campaign proposal framework of this plan was first used when I was a doctoral candidate and serving as the TA for the social media class taught by **Dr. Courtney Childers** at the University of Tennessee in 2011. We worked together throughout the class to determine the content and structure of the class and what needed to be incorporated into the class to make sure the students were prepared to handle this final project. I have taken this framework and updated and transformed it a bit by adding some additional requirements, added strategic sections, brand voice elements, etc.

SAMPLE SOCIAL MEDIA CAMPAIGN ASSIGMENT OVERVIEW

Your team will spend the remainder of the semester working towards the completion of a Social Media Plan for your client. You will submit an electronic copy to me via SafeAssign (by the team leader) and several hard copies (professionally bound and printed in color) to your professor by the deadline.

Title Page

Title of campaign with team names and group logo. Very visual and artistic. This needs to be formatted in landscape. This can be done in Word or in Adobe Illustrator as a PDF.

Bio of team members:

Professional pictures and format should be applied in this section.

Executive Summary

This is a one-page document that provides the reader a brief snapshot of your entire Social Media Plan.

Table of Contents

Headings for each key section need to be here along with the page numbers.

Introduction

Outline and research the particular industry your client is working for. For example, if you are working with the Louisville Bats team, you will need to make sure to account for what is happening in minor league baseball in terms of trends, etc. Look at local resources (Louisville Travel and Tourism), Census, Pew Research, etc for extra insights. You need to outline the environmental trends (ex. social media use, athletics, etc), social trends (ex. consumer behavior), technology trends (advancement of visual content, etc), and industry trends (ex. rise of influencers, content creation, etc) to paint a clear picture of what is going on in the industry your client is working in and what is happening in society.

Client Background
Include history of client, main personnel, its positioning, goals, mission, overall values and purpose. Report numbers for staff members, position of the client nationally / regionally / locally, popularity of feature content, the use of analytics for monitoring traffic), etc. It would probably be helpful to speak further to the client about other specifics you need – which you will get when the clients come to class.

Client Brand Voice Analysis
Overview of their overall brand voice based on tone, personality, consistency, content, level of engagement, etc. Highlight key attributes and characteristics associated with how they present themselves online.

Social media analysis
Includes previous campaigns they have done on social media, paid media, sponsored posts, influencer marketing, etc. Research into metrics, sentiment, engagement, influence levels need to be noted and cited here from your secondary research.

Competitor Analysis
Your team will identify primary, secondary and emerging competitors of your client. Outline what they are doing in the industry, location, social media space and what they are NOT doing so far in social media. Create an audit outlining their key profiles, what type of content they are doing, how long they have been active on each of the social media platforms, successful campaigns, overall brand voice they are projecting, and your overall conclusion for the brand online and how it compares with your client.

SWOT Analysis
You will conduct a one page SWOT Analysis for your client in regards to the competition. Further instruction will be provided about the layout of this page. You will be required to have some type of visual (probably a table) to compliment the explanation

provided in the full analysis. This will be a very important component in setting objectives and moving forward with Strategy and Tactics.

Audience Analysis
From the information provided in the client presentation, there seem to be many different opportunities for targeting. Make sure to have your primary key audiences listed and at least a couple secondary audiences. Key messages need to be aligned as well for each key audience based on their demographic, psychographic, social media use, current relationship with the client, expectations and motivational factors, influencers, and communication channel presence / voice expectation from the client.

Your team should analysis these audiences and provide insight into targeting implications. Provide numbers here. Be creative and make suggestions. Make sure to reference specific facts and statistics here in proper APA format.

Primary Research
All teams are required to conduct primary research. Your research plan does not have to be extensive and comprehensive. At minimum, your team should measure basic awareness of your client with potential audiences. The awareness percentage will serve as your baseline number for setting objectives and evaluating effectiveness of the proposed Social Media Plan overall.

Goals and Objectives
Listed below are some summarized five broad objectives that should guide your overall social media plan:

- Increase awareness of _____.
- Increase engagement with social media outlets.
- Educate internally _____ about the opportunities and impact of social media usage in promoting _____.

- Increase outreach and public partnerships for
  _____ within _____ communities.
- Influence positive perceptions of _____
  throughout the UofL campus and Louisville area.

Make sure you follow the SMART criteria for creating your
objectives (specific, measureable, achievable, realistic, and time-
specific). You and your team may have more additional objectives
here. There are just a few broad views of the needs/wants of your
client. How you work these into your strategy and tactics will set
you apart from the other teams in the course.

Strategy & Tactics

In some form or fashion, the following three topics must be
addressed:
- Analysis of Already Existing Social Media Use
- Critiques and Recommendations
- New strategies and tactics
- Rationale for new strategies and tactics

Budget
Provide an overview on how much this campaign will cost. You
will be able to get some of the key figures, but there are a few you
may need to estimate for the purpose of this assignment.

Calendar
You will need to create a calendar (Gantt Chart) for this proposal.
Outline all of the strategies, tactics, and measurement tools you
will be using for this campaign proposal.

Evaluation
The evaluation part of your social media plan is crucial. You need
to outline the steps you will be taking to make sure you have
accomplished the set objectives here for your social media plan.

Conclusion

Provide overview of plan, recommendations for future steps, and rationale on why this would work and be helpful for the campaign (1-2 paragraphs)

References (APA Style)

A list of secondary sources referenced in the text. You will need to provide all of the citations (ex. from reports, research, and other resources) here in alphabetical order in APA style. Check out this APA guide for reference:
http://owl.english.purdue.edu/owl/section/2/10/

Appendix

- Research Results (ex. transcripts, survey, etc)
- Suggested social media content (examples of visual content, Snapchat filters, etc)
- Timeline for content calendar
- Research and data analytics for campaign
- Breakdown for content creation and posting for an event
- List of resources

PRESENTATION OF THE FINAL PROPOSAL

- **Proposal:** You will be asked to create a professionally designed document for your social media campaign proposal (landscape layout). The professional design can be completed in a variety of programs: MS Word, Pages, InDesign or Illustrator, and Publisher, to name a few. It is up to your teams as to what program you choose for the professional layout.
- **Presentation:** Conversely, from experience, do not attempt to create this professional layout in PowerPoint, Photoshop, or Keynote.

ASSIGN GROUP MEMBERS TO GROUPS

I have heard this from a variety of different professors who have done a similar assignment for class. Some allow their students to choose their groups, while others assign them. I use research to assign each student to a particular group.

I do this for a variety of different reasons. First, sometimes friends are not the best to work with on a big group project. Second, you do not want all of the graphic designers to be in one group together. I try to gauge during the first week who is who by allowing the students to complete a survey (which I will only see) and then I use the data to assign the students into groups.

Once you have the groups outlined, you will want to designate a team leader and a co-leader (similar to a vice chair – someone who could step into the leader role if needed, but helps support the team leader). You also want to make sure to have each group member evaluate their group as a whole and add this as part of the overall assignment grade. I give my students the "three strikes" rule if there are any group members who are not active or helpful with the project. Here are my steps:

Progress/Peer Evaluations

In addition, starting the week _____, *the team leader* for each group will be asked to submit progress reports and evaluations to Dr. Freberg (karen.freberg@louisville.edu) via email. **This needs to be done each week (Friday at 5 pm EST).**

In the progress evaluations, you should explain what the responsibilities were for the social media plan during that week for each member, give insight as to how the team as a whole is performing, and share any positive or negative actions by other team members in regards to this project. Dr. Freberg will be the only people to view these individual progress evaluations. You will lose points on your individual score for the Social Media Plan if you do not submit the individual progress evals by the deadline (Friday at 5 p.m.) each week.

Also, be sure to include the week and number (example: Week 1), your name, and "Progress Evaluation" in the subject line. This will helps us with my records.

Evaluating your peers is an extremely important process in group work settings.

- I will read each progress evaluation thoroughly to try and identify problems before they spin out of control.
    - **First Step:** If a group is consistently having issues, we may see the need to hold an intervention-type team meeting.
    - **Second Step:** If a specific individual in the group continues to not perform and contribute to the team, we will hold an individual meeting with that team member.
    - **Third Step:** In this extreme case, I must be supportive of the decision. The "fired" team member will then have the chance to complete the assignment by him or herself or face a **0** for the entire Social Media Campaign project. If the student does the project by themselves, they will not be allowed to present the campaign to the client and will have to do the project on their own (not using resources from previous group). Highest grade possible will be a C on the project.

- Throughout the semester, we will watch closely to see whether the group or individual's evaluations become more positive in nature.

- If not, a second team meeting will be held. In the extreme case that a team member continues to do nothing to improve his/her contribution and participation, there will be the option of the team "firing" that member.
- Along with your peer evaluations, your clients will also be evaluating your performance on this class project as well. I will be taking these insights into consideration for the final project grade.

SECTION FEEDBACK

This is what has made my social media campaign proposals very successful for my students. I give them feedback on certain parts of their campaign proposal over the course of the semester.

The sections I have the groups turn into me for review include the background and research method section, midterm report (completed research and revised background section), strategies, tactics, and key messages, and evaluation + budget and calendar. Here are the feedback forms I give each group back related to each section:

Midterm Report for Social Media Campaign Proposal

This is a form where you can provide additional feedback and guidance for your student groups with their social media campaign proposal. The goal here is to provide them with a mock grade, essentially, to motivate them to do better in preparation for the final project at the end of the semester. You will want to provide them with enough feedback and comments to make sure they are aware of the expectations you have for them for their final project. Most of the students will need to have required revisions, but this will allow you to see where they are at a certain point in the semester as well as what they need to work on. Each group could have different strengths and challenges. Once you have completed this form, you will need to send this to all of the group members for their review. Ask them to let you know they have received this feedback and will incorporate this into their final project. This can also be sent directly to the group leader as well.

MIDTERM FEEDBACK FORM
Team Leader:
Team Members:
Client:

MIDTERM REPORT FEEDBACK AND GRADING NOTES

	FEEDBACK	RECOMMENDED CHANGES 1 - REQUIRED => 3 RECOMMENDED => NO CHANGE
INDUSTRY OVERVIEW	•	
RESEARCH METHOD AND QUESTIONS	•	
AUDIENCE ANALYSIS	•	
SWOT ANALYSIS	•	
SOCIAL MEDIA AUDIT	•	
QUALITY OF WRITING + REFERENCES	•	
ADDITIONAL COMMENTS	•	
MIDTERM GRADE (MOCK GRADE)	•	
PROFESSOR RECOMMENDATIONS	•	

STRATEGIES AND TACTICS FEEDBACK FORM

This is a form where you can provide additional feedback and guidance for your student groups with their strategies and tactics section for their social media campaign proposal. The goal here is to provide them with a mock grade, essentially, to motivate them to do better in preparation for the final project at the end of the semester. This is essentially the heart and soul of their proposal (based on the points for the final proposal assignment).

You will want to provide them with enough feedback and comments to make sure they are aware of the expectations you have for them for their final project. Most of the students will need to have required revisions, but this will allow you to see where they are at a certain point in the semester as well as what they need to work on. Each group could have different strengths and challenges. Once you have completed this form, you will need to send this to all of the group members for their review. Ask them to let you know they have received this feedback and will incorporate this into their final project. This can also be sent directly to the group leader as well.

STRATEGIES AND TACTICS FEEDBACK FORM

Team Leader:
Team Members:
Client:

	FEEDBACK	RECOMMENDED CHANGES 1 - REQUIRED => 3 RECOMMENDED => NO CHANGE
OVERVIEW OF STRATEGIES AND TACTICS	•	•
ALIGNMENT TO GOALS AND OBJECTIVES	•	•
ANALYSIS OF CREATIVE STRATEGIES	•	•
COMPETITIVE ANALYSIS OF STRATEGIES	•	•
SOCIAL MEDIA VISUAL CONTENT EXAMPLES FOR STRATEGIES AND TACTICS	•	•
QUALITY OF WRITING + REFERENCES	•	•
PRESENTATION / PROFESSIONALISM OF CONTENT	•	•
ADDITIONAL COMMENTS	•	•
STRATEGIES AND TACTICS GRADE (MOCK GRADE)		
PROFESSOR RECOMMENDATIONS		

	D or below [Unsatisfactory]	C [Satisfactory]	B [Proficient]	A [Exceptional]	SCORE
ORGANIZATION & ASSIGNMENT STYLE [20 points]	No organization or structure.	Postings provide minimal insights and understanding on topic. Little reflection and creativity present. Provides minimal research and evidence.	Postings provide moderate insight and understanding with integration of creativity interwoven into commentary. Provides moderate evidence and research	Paper provide comprehensive understanding, insights, commentary, and focuses on bringing forth new questions, new ideas, and sparks conversation to extend the discussion in the community. Provides extensive list of resources and evidence.	
STRATEGIC INSIGHT AND BACKGROUND RESEARCH + ANALYSIS [60 points]	Poor research (primary and secondary) + analysis of competitor social media presence / SWOT analysis. Detail for each section is not acceptable at this level.	Minimum research (primary and secondary) + basic analysis of competitor social media presence / SWOT analysis. Detail for each section is present but done at the minimal level of expectations.	Good research (primary and secondary) + nice analysis of competitor social media presence / SWOT analysis. Detail for each section is present, but could be a bit stronger.	Strategic understanding is strongly presented throughout the post and done in a professional and integrated manner. Author is very careful in selecting appropriate words to fit commentary and subject. Strong research (primary and secondary) + thorough analysis of competitor social media presence / SWOT analysis	
ALIGNMENT TO GOALS AND OBJECTIVES [40 points]	No alignment or rationale for tie ins to the SWOT analysis and previous sections Not connected at all to proposed goals and objectives	Goals and objectives are slightly mentioned, but not fully connected or aligned. Rationale for connection to goals and objectives are not strong but mentioned.	Goals and objectives are somewhat connected, but there are some missing components that could be strengthened. Rationale for why these strategies are connected are good. Some connection to previous research and competitor analysis.	Excellent connection and alignment for the goals and objectives from the previous research + competitive analysis. Mentions the "so what factor" and strategic implications Strategies and tactics fit perfectly within the overall paper and are backed up with strong evidence and rationale.	
CREATIVE + STRATEGIC CONTENT [40 points]	Does not insert any images or graphics, images may not be appearing correctly, does not acknowledge source or provide a caption	Inserts graphics and multimedia, but not of high quality. Has some captions, but no hyperlinks and not for all sources	Inserts graphics and multimedia of high quality, infographics. Has captions for sources.	Selects and inserts high quality graphics with captions and hyperlinks to the sources. Acknowledges all sources of content. Creates own infographic and graphics.	
EVALUATION AND MEASUREMENT [40 points]	No measurement or evaluation concluded, Only included vanity metrics. No alignment to KPIS and objectives	Measurement and evaluation are conducted with minimal metrics listed and minimal proposed evaluation tools and methods. KPIs did not	Measurement and evaluation are conducted with good list of key metrics and KPIs and as well as proposed evaluation tools and	Excellent and thorough analysis, recommendation, and connection for the measurement and evaluation. KPIs are aligned with the	

This is a form where you can provide your analysis and final grades for your student groups with their social media campaign proposal. This will let the students know what they received for their final grades as a group for their presentation, proposal, and initial feedback from the clients.

SOCIAL MEDIA CAMPAIGNS GROUP FEEDBACK FORM [260 PTS]

Team Leader:
Team Members:
Group Name:
Client:

RUBRIC FOR SOCIAL MEDIA FINAL CAMPAIGN PROPOSAL

	with tools and methods proposed.	tie in strongly to methods and objectives. No rationale is mentioned for why to use these tools and metrics.	methods. Brief rationale for why to use these metrics and tools. Suggestions for future campaigns and measurement are listed.	objectives and appropriate tools, methods, and services for each platform and the rationale for why it is key to use these. Suggestions for future campaigns and measurement are listed
CALENDAR, BUDGET, AND APPENDIX [30 points]	No budget, calendar, summary or appendix presented	Minimal presence of budget, calendar, and appendix. Issues pertaining to the timing and cost associated with the budget.	Good overview of the key elements in the budget and calendar. Missing calculations and professional branding.	Extremely thorough content analysis and calendar. Organized through strategies and tactics. Perfect calculations.	
CITATIONS AND RESOURCES [20 points]	No citations or image citations as well as no reading list. Citations are not present or in the current format.	Minimal amount of citations required (20). Reading list is <5. Issues with citation format in paper for consistency.	Moderate amount of citations (30). Provides a reading list for more resources (10). Good citations with a few mistakes.	Extensive amount of citations and hyperlinks to relevant articles, reports, and resources on subject. Provides an extensive amount of reading posts for readers (40+).	
QUALITY OF WRITING AND PROOFREADING [20 points]	The writing is confused and/or ungrammatical. The reporting is flawed and may contain major factual errors and/or omissions or may show little concept of basic strategic judgment. Work may miss the deadline. Many grammatical and spelling errors, punctuation errors, and text message lingo. Style does not facilitate professionalism or effective communication	This grade is for work that indicates a problem in at least one area, such as grammar, diplomacy or strategy. It does not measure up to professional quality but could be saved by revision. Work is incomplete by deadline and/or needs more than minor revision. These messages have weak ideas, concepts or presentation. Minimal grammar and spelling errors. Style is more conversational and may distract from the reader.	Writing is grammatically correct but may lack the sparkle and fine organization of "A" work. The work is turned in by deadline with little or no prompting and needs only minor revisions in such areas as reorganizing, rewriting, reformatting or providing more or better sources.	This grade is for work of clearly professional quality (publishable or broadcast ready). The writing is clear and well-organized; presentation and nearly flawless writing. No grammar or spelling errors. Strong writing that helps facilitate strong communication and dialogue.	
TOTAL SCORE					

11 SAMPLE SYLLABUS FOR A SOCIAL MEDIA CLASS

You now have all of the assignments to teach a social media class on your own. Now, how do you go about organizing these into one single document for a class? How do I outline what areas to cover on which day? How many points am I going to give out for each assignment?

That's where this section comes in. This is another document I have not shared openly, but in this case, I am happy to do so. I have included my syllabus for my social media class so you can see my policies, what books I have assigned to the class, and what additional readings I have.

Here are some things to keep in mind when you are creating your class and syllabus:

- *Interview students before they can enroll in class.* You want to make sure they realize this is a hard class to take. Many students assume you will only be tweeting and snapping in a social media class. I share my 30+ page syllabus with my students during this interview and ask them – do you feel you can commit to this class and the work? I haven't had a student tell me "no" yet.
- *Visuals are always good to have here:* Make sure to have pictures of the books, resources, and assignments for the class (ex. Hootsuite).
- *Be prepared for students talking negatively about the work and readings:* I get this sometimes from students and this is one thing I stress at the beginning of the semester – you will at times not like this class, but it will all pay off at the end of the semester. If you convey the benefits and skills they will be able to get from this, they will do the work.
- *Have professionals review your syllabus.* My syllabus has been vetted through a variety of different groups, but mostly professionals. Ask local and national professionals you know who would give you some good insight about what to cover for your social media class.

- *Have required AND recommended books (and resources):* I have both here for the class – the goal is to have enough resources for the students to be able to get a grasp of what the field is all about.

Note, for the readings in the tentative schedule section, I do have them available via the Hootlet URL shortner, which I have found to be very helpful for my students. I also make sure to include the Twitter handle for my guest speakers so my students can connect with them online before their presentations.

SAMPLE SOCIAL MEDIA CLASS SYLLABUS

Course Description

Social media, Mobile Technologies and Strategic Communications (COMM 333) will be an upper-level course dedicated to exploring the new emerging technologies and mediums influencing business, marketing, public relations, and advertising practices and research.

This course will acquaint you with practical knowledge and analytical skills necessary to create, evaluate, and execute social media and mobile campaigns. This course will also provide lectures, iconic and current case studies using social media and mobile, group and individual assignments, and engaged activities that will help you in developing a strong social media skill set to take to future job and/or internship interviews in your respective field of study.

COURSE PREREQUISITES & RECOMMENDATIONS

COMM 342 (Introduction to Strategic Communications). If you have not taken COMM 342 before, please see me as soon as possible.

STUDENT LEARNING OUTCOMES

This course will acquaint you with practical knowledge and analytical skills necessary to create, evaluate, and execute social media campaigns. **COMM 333** will provide lectures, case studies, assignments, and engaged activities that will help you in developing a strong social media skill set to take to future job and/or internship interviews in your respective field of study.

At the end of this course, you will be able to:

- Provide insight about and experience with current and emerging social media tools and digital technologies;
- Have knowledge about various opportunities for strategically implementing digital, social, and mobile media into strategic communication practices and research;
- Understand the importance of managing online personal reputation and a business/organization's identity through social media applications;
- Provide awareness of ethical, legal, and privacy issues when using social media outlets;
- Be able to listen, participating in, and monitoring online conversations in a professional and strategic manner;
- Present insights and strategies related to social media implementation and best practices;
- Connecting theory and application of social media marketing and the strategic decisions made prior to the implementation of social media and mobile technologies;
- Awareness and understanding of the need for research and evaluation when incorporating social media in an overall IMC campaign.

COURSE COMMITMENT

By enrolling in this class, you are making a strong commitment to this course, your peers, your professor, and yourself. This class should present a more engaging student experience -- both inside and outside of the classroom -- than what you might have experienced in courses before.

We will use social media tools to be interactive with one another throughout this semester. Active participation with the course Blackboard site is imperative, as you should check Blackboard each day before coming to class.

All assignment details will be distributed via Blackboard. I will use the class email communication tool or the announcements feature on Blackboard for all major announcements.

MEASUREMENT OF COURSE OBJECTIVES

This course will use various assignments to complete and measure the course objectives. The breakdown of the assignments for this course is listed below:

Participation & Attendance (In class)	10%
Social media participation	10%
Snapchat/Live Streaming/Emerging Media Assignment	10%
Hootsuite Higher Education Certification Program	15%
Blogging Assignment	15%
Managing Online Reputation Paper	10%
Social Media Campaign Proposal	30%
TOTAL	**100%**

Social Media Participation
You will also need to make sure you are sharing your weekly blog posts as well on Twitter with the class hashtag. **NOTE:** All weekly tweets should **NOT** be done all at the same time (ex. Friday morning). Participation points will reflect this – these need to be completed over the course of the week in class to get full engagement from the class community.

Hootsuite Assignment
For this class, everyone will be participating in the Hootsuite Higher Education program. Hootsuite is a social media dashboard that allows individuals and brands to monitor, listen, and engage with their audiences across multiple platforms in a centralized location.

More information about the program can be found at: www.learn.hootsuite.com. It is also recommended to follow Hootsuite University on Twitter during this course (@Hootsuite). You will also want to make sure to follow Kimberly Yu (@kimhoots) and Kelsey Wong (@kelseyhoots) – they are the main contacts for Hootsuite. At the beginning of the semester, you will be receiving an email from Hootsuite to get access to your free Hootsuite Pro account for 90 days. This is part of the certification program. The program involves several exams as well as a library of lessons about Hootsuite components and features, trends involving social media monitoring, and lessons on how to apply Hootsuite in your social media strategy plans for clients.

Once you have completed the certification program, you will be able to get a widget to embed on your class blog as well as be listed in their Hootsuite Certified Professionals & Social Media Consultants database (http://learn.hootsuite.com/social-media-consultants).

Remember, you have to make sure to access the initial email by Hootsuite University in **24 hours** to get into your account. Otherwise, your password will be expired.

For this assignment, you will need to 1) complete the Hootsuite University exams and watch the videos with the downloadable workbooks as part of the certification program, 2) announcing your certification in social media once you have completed Hootsuite University and received the official notification with the class hashtag **#Freberg16,** and 3) create a reflection post in Adobe Page Spark along with a reaction blog post about your experience with Hootsuite and lessons learned from the experience. You will need to turn in a hard copy of all of these documents for this assignment.

Blogging Assignment

One of the more established forms of online media presently among advertising and public relations professionals are blogs. Some have even considered them to be more like traditional media. For this semester, you will be creating your own personal blog where you will be asked to write posts relevant to course material, current events happening in the industry, and other topics of interest to you.

Blogs should be an interactive, current, and engaging platform where you can show and demonstrate your visual, written, and creative expertise about a particular subject of interest.

This is also a place where you are sharing your insights and education with the online community. These blogs should allow you to showcase your knowledge and experience in StratComm, while also reflecting a positive, energetic, and dynamic reputation as a young professional / student.

For this semester, you will be asked to create a blog and maintain for this class. You will be writing insightful, well-researched, and thorough blog posts on topics related to social media in strategic communications.

Snapchat / Live Streaming / Emerging Media Strategic Storytelling Assignment

You will be asked to create and present a brief for a strategic storytelling proposal for Snapchat, Livestreaming (Periscope or Meerkat), or an emerging new platform that has launched recently during the time of this class.

If you would like to do all of these options, you are more than welcome to do so as well for extra credit. However, if you do, you have to do a proposed analytics report for Snapchat, Meerkat, and Periscope in addition.

Social Media Group Project Plan

Students will be working in teams of four-five creating a campaign for a client selected by the instructor. The details of this assignment will be provided during the first weeks of the semester. Each individual assignment for this class will prepare students with this campaign proposal and presentation. The report is worth **20%** of the grade and the final presentation is worth **10%**. The final presentations will be held during finals week. Your clients and local professionals will be in attendance. You will also be required to do peer evaluations as well – which will be a factor for your overall individual grade for this assignment.

EMAIL & SOCIAL MEDIA ETIQUETTE

Professional email and social media correspondence both a key factor and component not only for this class, but also for your future job prospects after graduation. Setting a good first impression with your email and social media writing is key. Treat each email, tweet, snap, and update as you would if you were working at an agency or for a brand. Today, it's essential to have strong social media and email etiquette skills because this is what is expected in the workplace.

First impressions based on your email or other electronic forms of communication is essential and can make/break opportunities for you in your future jobs, internships, and other professional opportunities. It is always best to be professional and respectful for all correspondence – **especially in this course**.

Please be professional when writing emails to the instructor – and make sure that correct spelling and grammar is used. Put your name and the title of the class in the subject line. I will respond to emails as soon as possible. Make sure to <u>check your University Email daily & Class Twitter hashtag a couple of times a day</u>. You can work with the HelpDesk to have your University email forwarded to an account you already check daily.

Other things to keep in mind for our class this semester:

- **Professional Format:** Please be professional when writing emails to the instructor – and make sure that correct spelling and grammar is used. Put your name and the title of the class in the subject line. I will respond to emails as soon as possible in at least 24 hours during the week, and at least 48 hours during the weekend.
- **Boundaries:** We are indeed working in a 24/7 industry and environment today, but we also have to be respectful to each other's boundaries when it comes to expectations of replies, timing of responses, etc. This goes for not only the professor for this class, but also for professionals working in the industry.
- **Golden Rule for Writing Professionally is about RESPECT:** If you wouldn't write an email or tweet to your boss for your dream job or internship, then do not write it to me. Treat this class as you would in your dream job with your boss and fellow colleagues. If you treat me with respect in your writing and correspondence for class, I will do the same for you.
- **Timing of Emails:** I will **NOT** answer emails/tweets that are forwarded or RTed to try to get higher on my email list. / Twitter feed. One email or tweet is efficient and appropriate. I will respond to emails in a timely manner. This means at least in the span of 24 hours, not 24 minutes. If you email me at 3 am, don't expect an immediate response.
- **Addressing the Professor:** Please address the email as Dr. Freberg or Professor Freberg. I will not respond to emails that do not start off with this introduction or addressing me as Karen. This also is key for social media correspondence as well.

- **Proper Spelling and Grammar for Email and Social Media:** Make sure to check for spelling and grammar – if I see a spelling/grammar mistake, I will either not answer the email or grade the email as part of your participation grade for this course.
- **Emojis and Text Lingo**: No emojis or text lingo in email correspondence with the professor. Emojis are okay if professional on social media correspondence for the class.
- **Email signatures:** Create a professional signature for your email address. Even if you are typing from an iPhone / iPad / Surface / Android / etc.
- **Resources:** Email Etiquette from <u>Purdue Owl</u> and Social Media <u>Resources</u> & Guides

SOCIAL MEDIA ETIQUETTE

- **Public Forum:** We will be using social media for our outside class participation, so this is a public forum for everyone and ANYONE can read your tweets. Be aware of these before you tweet, update, or even snap for class.
- **Respect:** Be respectful and professor for everyone in class, including the professor.
- **Check spelling and grammar**: Make sure you are double-checking the spelling and grammar for all of your updates, even the class hashtag. Otherwise, we will not be able to see your tweets related to the class.
- **Live tweeting or updating in class;** Unless specified, you should not be on your phone and on social media. Especially when we have guest speakers unless the guest speakers say it is okay or the professor says it is okay. If you are on your phone during class time and not paying attention to the course material, you will 1) miss out on important information related to the class and 2) this will show disrespect to your fellow classmates, the professor, and the guest speaker.
- **Timing:** I will try to respond in at least 24 hours for email and maybe a few hours at the latest for social media updates. Don't 1) forward me your email if I have not responded in an hour, 2) email and tweet me about the same questions – I will answer in one format or another depending on the scope of the question and 3) Don't expect an immediate answer if you are tweeting an immediate concern at 3 am – I will respond to this later in the morning.

Readings

There is an argument on whether or not to "assign" a book for a social media class. Some classes do, but others do not. I am in the mindset of having a foundational book is key, and it helps build the student's library of work as they enter the workplace.

With that being said, it is important to make sure to add current and relevant articles along with the chapter readings for the students. I use these articles to share current news articles, case studies, resources that may be applicable for a particular platform, etc. These can be added to the course readings by simply creating a shortened URL link through Hootlet (or Bitly so you can track stats) like this if I was covering Snapchat for class (you will want to add at least 3-5 articles like this for each class meeting for the students).

- Snapchat lacks one of Instagram's key to success - Business Insider http://www.businessinsider.com/snapchat-lacks-one-of-instagrams-key-to-success-2016-8
- How to Create and Use Snapchat's New Custom Geofilters https://www.garyvaynerchuk.com/how-to-create-and-use-snapchats-new-custom-geofilters/

12 ADDITIONAL RESOURCES

So, we have the assignments to teach a social media class and we have the syllabus. However, we all know social media changes quickly and every day. How do we keep up with the evergrowing changes in the industry and adapt them to our syllabus and class?

In addition to these assignments, here are some resources and accounts you may want to follow to keep up to date on what is happening in social media.

SOCIAL MEDIA RESOURCES

Additional social media resources for readings will be posted on Blackboard. Here are a list of useful sites to follow on a daily basis to get the latest trends and issues regarding new emerging technologies:

SOCIAL MEDIA PROS	SOCIAL MEDIA & SPORTS	PR PROFESSIONALS	BRANDS
o @TedRubin	o @ChrisYandle	o @dbreakenridge	o @TACOBELL
o @MarkWSchaefer	o @Jonathan_Gantt	o @shonaliburke	o @KYDERBY
o @garyvee	o @CUJeffKallin	o @armano	o @UNDERARMOUR
o @JayBaer	o @WarJessEagle	o @wadds	o @STARBUCKS
o @MariSmith	o @BrianRWagner	o @melissa_agnes	o @DUNKINDONUTS
o @DennisYu	o @digitalruss	o @scottmonty	o @XGAMES
o @leeodden	o @JoeyMaestras	o @EdelmanPR	o @GOPRO
o @Britopian	o @samanthahughey	o @FleishmanHillard	o @COCACOLA
o @JasonFalls	o @jeremydarlow	o @Digiday	o @CASPER
o @chriskerns	o @MichaelElhrich	o @Social@Ogilvy	o @OREO
o @DJWaldrow	o @fieldhousemedia	o @247LS	o @LARAMS
o @TheTimHayden	o @KevinDeShazo	o @Droga5	o @HOOTSUITE
o @nickcicero	o @tariq_ahmad	o @Vaynermedia	o @SPROUTSOCIAL
o @UFC_Shanda	o @SportTechie	o @ESPNPR	o @BUFFER
o @Ober	o @fntofficesports	o @EDELMANAR	o @ADOBE
o @JenniHogan	o @ksvobada		o @ZIGNALLABS
o @kcote	o @Mark_Hodgkin		o @MLS
	o @jskarp		o @TEAMUSA
	o @frntofficesport		o @CLEMSONATHLETICS
	o @GenYDigital		o @SEAHAWKS
			o @UFC
			o @NBA

WEBSITES	BLOGS	PRACTITIONERS
• Advertising Age – Digital Next: http://adage.com/digitalnext/	• Advertising Age – Digital Next: http://adage.com/digitalnext/	• Chris Brogan: http://chrisbrogan.com/
• Ragan Communications PR Daily Newsletter: http://prdaily.com	• Ragan Communications PR Daily Newsletter: http://prdaily.com	• Gary Vaynerchuck: https://www.garyvaynerchuk.com/
• Spreadfast Blog: https://www.spredfast.com/social-marketing-blog	• Spreadfast Blog: https://www.spredfast.com/social-marketing-blog	• Jason Falls: http://www.jasonfalls.com/
• Hootsuite Blog: http://www.blog.hootsuite.com	• Hootsuite Blog: http://www.blog.hootsuite.com	• Stephen Waddington: http://wadds.co.uk/
• Buffer Blog: http://blog.bufferapp.com/	• Buffer Blog: http://blog.bufferapp.com/	• Jessica Smith: http://socialnsport.com/
• Social Media Explorer: http://www.socialmediaxplorer.com/	• Social Media Explorer: http://www.socialmediaexplorer.com/	• Ann Handley: http://www.marketingprofs.com/
• AdAge (Digital): http://adage.com	• AdAge (Digital): http://adage.com	• Jason Falls: http://www.socialmediaexplorer.com/
• AdWeek: http://www.adweek.com	• AdWeek: http://www.adweek.com	• Deirdre Breakenridge: http://www.deirdrebreakenridge.com/
• Fast Company: http://www.fastcompany.com	• Fast Company: http://www.fastcompany.com	• David Armano: http://darmano.typepad.com/
• Social Media Today: http://www.socialmediatoday.com	• Social Media Today: http://www.socialmediatoday.com	• Scott Monty: http://www.scottmonty.com/
	• Business 2 Community: http://www.business2community.com	• Jay Baer: http://www.convinceandconvert.com/
	• Mashable: http://www.mashable.com	• Kyle Lacy: http://kylelacy.com/
	• PR Squared: http://www.pr-squared.com/	• Melissa Agnes: http://agnesday.com/
	• Techcrunch:	• Mark Schaefer: http://www.businessesgrow.com/
		• Jonathan Bernstein: http://www.bernsteincrisismanagement.com/

- Business 2 Community: http://www.business2community.com
- Mashable: http://www.mashable.com
- PR Squared: http://www.pr-squared.com/
- Digiday: www.digiday.com
- Edelman PR: http://edelmandigital.com/page/1/
- Ignite Social Media: http://www.ignitesocialmedia.com/blog/
- Delmondo: http://delmondo.co/
- WeAreSocial: http://wearesocial.com/
- Droga5: http://droga5.com/
- Social@Oglivy: https://social.ogilvy.com/
- Razorfish: http://www.razorfish.com/
- Vaynermedia: http://vaynermedia.com/ & Grapestory: http://www.grapestory.co/

- http://techcrunch.com/
- NextWeb: http://thenextweb.com/
- DigitalBuzz Blog: http://www.digitalbuzzblog.com/
- Zignal Labs: http://zignallabs.com/blog/
- Laundry Service: http://tumblr.247laundryservice.com/
- Golin: http://golin.com/
- SHIFT Communications: http://www.shiftcomm.com/blog/
- 360i Blog: http://blog.360i.com/

Keep in mind, social media constantly changes each and every day, so this assignment ebook will be updated as new platforms, tools, and assignments come available. If you want to reach out to me directly if you have questions or comments about any of the assignments, please email me at karen.freberg@louisville.edu, or connect with me on social media at @kfreberg.

ABOUT THE AUTHOR

Karen Freberg (@kfreberg) is an assistant professor in Strategic Communications at the University of Louisville. In addition to this teaching experience, Freberg has presented at several U.S. and international research conferences, including ones in Australia, Brazil, China, Greece, Italy, Slovenia, Spain, Sweden, and The Netherlands.

In addition, Freberg's social media pedagogy practices has been featured in *Forbes* and in *USA Today College* publications.

Freberg is also a research consultant in social media and crisis communications and has worked with several organizations and agencies such as Firestorm Solutions, Hootsuite, DHS, CDC, National Center for Food Protection and Defense (NCFPD), and the Colorado Ski Association. In 2015, Freberg was named as a Plank Educator Fellow where she was able to spend time at General Motors working with them on social media analytics and influencer relations. Freberg's research has been published in several book chapters and in academic journals such as *Public Relations Review, Media Psychology Review, Journal of Contingencies and Crisis Management and Health Communication.* She also serves on the editorial board for *Psychology for Popular Media Culture, Corporate Communication: An International Journal, Journal of Public Relations Research*, and *Case Studies in Strategic Communication* (CSSC).

Before coming to the University of Louisville, Freberg earned a PhD in Communication and Information at the University of Tennessee in May 2011, and a Master's degree in Strategic Public Relations at the Annenberg School for Communication at the University of Southern California in August 2007. Freberg received her Bachelor's of Science degree in Public Relations at the University of Florida in August 2005.

Made in the USA
Middletown, DE
13 October 2016